MELONS to MONEY

Growing Food, Lives & Social Enterprise

GAYLE PINCUS

ISBN-13:9781484934074
ISBN-10:1484934075

Library of Congress Control Number: 2013909194
CreateSpace Independent Publishing Platform
North Charleston, South Carolina

Dedicated to Lauren and Nicki who have both
chosen careers of extraordinary social purpose

PREFACE

Who should read this book?

Have you ever wondered how some nonprofits are harvesting the rewards from well-run social enterprises? If you've ever wondered, "How do they do that?" then this book is for you.

Melons to Money is an inspirational story and a guide for anyone in the nonprofit sector considering earned income revenues. This includes nonprofit CEOs, executive directors, and board members who recognize that the financial sustainability of their nonprofit organization is imperative. You might also be a student participating in nonprofit curriculums, or any one of the increasing numbers of social entrepreneurs who want to make a real difference in the world. The goal of this book is to build your confidence, knowledge, and insight for launching a social purpose business.

This is a story about a young CEO who successfully plans and implements a social enterprise—but not without a few realistic struggles, like making the next payroll. Even though the story is fiction, it is grounded in a realistic setting and in realistic economic conditions.

The enterprise of NextPlace4Good employs clients of its nonprofit organization in an urban garden and a Farmer's Market located in a low income community. Besides generating profit, their most important goal is workforce development. *Your* goal might also include reducing barriers to employment for your clients. But revenue diversification, increasing unrestricted funds, and leveraging an unmet market need are also great reasons to consider a social purpose business. The common goal of any social enterprise is to produce a mission-based, predictable, and profitable stream of revenue.

How should the book be read and used?

This is a story. It's intended to be read over a weekend, on a plane, at the beach, or in any relaxed setting. The story is organized into sections or phases of development from readiness to completion. The sections are noted in the Table of Contents and throughout the story. An aspiring social entrepreneur or enterprising nonprofit organization can see what might happen during each phase.

The story format makes reading this book about social enterprise a more engaging way to think about business planning, while also explaining and answering important questions such as the following:

- What should I do first?
- Why do I need a business plan?
- What does a business plan look like?
- How do I understand the marketplace for our idea?
- What resources and expertise should we have?

And there's one more important benefit to this book. The format embeds a process in the story. This practical business planning process removes the mystique of business planning for those without business backgrounds. It provides a common framework and language for teams, including those with strong business backgrounds. As a reader, you'll easily internalize the way to think about a business plan: first, understand the market opportunity; second, develop the initiative to meet a market need; and third, translate the initiative's words into a financial model.

This three-step planning process will result in more successful financing and a better chance at succeeding as an enterprise. When a tax exempt organization engages me as their business advisor, I use this straightforward process. Everyone gets it, and the process creates really wonderful enterprises.

Something else to keep in mind: the story I tell in this book about a model social enterprise emphasizes the time these nonprofit leaders took to understand the market opportunity for their enterprise. In many cases tax exempt organizations don't need to complete a market analysis because there's always a waiting list of people to serve beyond their capacity to serve them. When an organization starts planning a social business venture, however, customers will choose where to spend their money, so leaders *must* understand the characteristics of their market and where to target and deeply understand a specific customer segment of that market.

Once the planning team has developed a clear understanding of its target market, it becomes much easier to see how to organize the business enterprise—to define the initiative and the gaps that need filling, as well as find ways to eliminate or mitigate risks. Once the planning team has discussed the initiative, the financial model can be constructed.

Throughout the story I tell, you'll see excerpts of planning and financial documents inserted into the text, but only those excerpts necessary to keep the story moving. Readers interested in the completed business plan can refer to Part 2.

Why did I write this book?

I wrote this story for three reasons: to encourage and inspire nonprofit leaders who have the glimmer of an idea for earned income, to share how it's done in an interesting way, and to promote business planning!

I feel strongly about business planning. If you don't do it, you'll end up somewhere, but it may not be where you wanted to be. As a business consultant, I often hear people say things like, "We don't need no stinkin' business plan. Let's just do it. Ready, fire, aim!"

In contrast, my book provides you a model for constructing a business plan that is discussed, developed, and agreed upon by multiple stakeholders, leveraging all their skills. The key implementers understand the essence of the strategy and the plan and can act accordingly. They don't need to read someone's mind or centralize all decisions to a single person. And as Michael, a successful retired businessman, says at the story's conclusion, "The more we plan, the smarter we get." That's been my experience, too.

One caution--there is a skill you gain through practice of knowing when enough planning is enough. That is the value of having someone with business planning experience on the planning team.

Doesn't the social sector need earned income as an ingredient to a financially sustainable business model? Look at our situation. As citizens, we ask nonprofit, tax exempt organizations to deliver goods and services to people living in our communities who are in need. How are we doing? Not well. Significant, unmet needs continue to increase in an environment of shrinking government resources and growing competition for charitable donations.

I congratulate prudent, responsible nonprofits that provide services to clients at the level the organization can afford and sustain. But how do we create a business model that can sustainably grow the number of people who receive the services? And how can we better expand services to *all* who need them?

One clear answer is through social enterprise, which can augment a nonprofit organization's more traditional revenues from donors, events, and grants. I wrote this story to encourage and support your efforts to expand and diversify your revenue stream. My hope is that it brings high value to you and your enterprise.

Gayle Pincus
May 2013

ACKNOWLEDGEMENTS

I wrote a story as a way to communicate the value of social enterprise. I think this is an engaging way to share a meaningful business planning process. As this is my first work of fiction, I greatly appreciate the feedback of colleagues who read versions of *Melons to Money* and provided valuable insights on how to make the story more interesting and the situations more believable. My gratitude goes to Nora Hannah, Michael McCaffrey, Patrick McWhorter, Will Neitzke and Elliott Rachlin for their comments, suggestions and encouragement.

Many thanks to the clients who worked with me and with this process to launch their successful enterprises. It was a win for them and at the same time gave me confidence that the business planning process described in the story is a great fit for social purpose businesses. Special thanks to St. Luke's Health Initiatives, Phoenix, AZ for funding research on healthy food distribution models in low income communities. I continued the initial research to learn more about good practices for growing melons and fresh produce for sale at Farmer's Markets.

Now, two years after beginning this project, I realize how important it's been to have my support network of Shea Group executives and business owners who have provided encouragement and advice. One Shea Group member has to be put on a pedestal. Will Neitzke sat patiently with me each week, and provided awesome insight to every aspect of the book. Thank you so much Will!

The book is all the more interesting to read after the capable editing of Dr. Laura L. Bush. And if you own the book it's with the able assistance of fellow author and word-of-mouth marketing architect Ann Videan.

My thanks go to my extended family and daughters Lauren and Nicki for their unconditional love and, in particular to my husband, Steve who has been fantastically supportive during my entire career.

TABLE OF CONTENTS

PART 1:

WHERE SOCIAL PURPOSE MEETS BUSINESS

SECTION 1:
Getting Ready

Never Let a Good Crisis Go To Waste

The late model silver Jaguar glides into an open parking space between the beat-up early model Hondas and Toyotas. The driver, a 60-year-old in a Navy blazer, open button-down blue shirt and corporate gray slacks walks toward the door, arriving at the same time as a very pregnant young woman. He holds the door for her as she enters the building.

"Do you know where the clothes room is?" she asks. Michael is flustered, but there isn't anyone else in the reception area to ask, so he offers to help.

"The *close* room? Could you say again what you're looking for?"

"I came for the clothes room they have here. I need some baby clothes for when my baby girl is born."

"Oh-h!" Michael says, making the connection, and then looking around the reception area for a *Clothes Room* sign. A younger man bounds into the reception area, his hand outreached to greet Michael. Then he turns to the woman, "Hello, I'm Jason Greene. I'm the CEO of NextPlace4Good. How can I help you?"

Repeating her question to Jason, he tells her that office hours ended at 5:00 p.m. and no one is staffing the *Clothes Room* until tomorrow. Her shoulders drop; she bites her lower lip. Seeing her dejection, Jason realizes he is overly focused on his new board member's visit.

"Michael, if it's okay, let me see if one of my staff can help this young woman while she's here."

"Sure, Jason. No problem. I'm brand new to the board of NextPlace4Good, and since I'm here to see the facility, the *Clothes Room* can be the first stop on my tour."

"Great! And, I apologize. I neglected to get your name."

"Malaika" she answers. "This is the only day I could leave work early. I had to walk a long way from the bus. I got here as soon as I could. I'm sorry I got here after you closed."

"That's alright. Both of you can come with me. We'll find some nice clothes for your baby, Malaika, and give Michael a tour of NextPlace4Good at the same time."

As the three walk down the hall, Michael asks Malaika where she works.

"At the McDonalds on 32nd Street and Shea Boulevard."

He tries to imagine how she might have travelled the cross-town distance to this facility, including walking the last mile, probably from downtown Phoenix, very pregnant after a full workday. Michael thinks to himself, "This is who we help."

Realizing how difficult life must be for Malaika to meet her basic needs, Michael makes a mental note to pay a taxi for her ride home. Does she have a home? Another mental note: "Talk to Jason. Get his advice on how to approach paying for the taxi."

Michael continues the conversation, "I know that McDonald's. I took my children there when they were little. Have you worked there a long time?"

"Almost a year. I was lucky they were hiring. I looked for a job for six months and no one was hiring during the recession. At least my boyfriend kept his job."

The three of them stopped at the doorway of a large room. The walls were lined with mismatched bedroom dressers and several racks of hanging clothes. Jason walked to a dresser marked "baby clothes" and showed Malaika where to start looking.

"Since I have an appointment with Michael, I'll find one of my staff members to finish helping you, Malaika. You take care of yourself and have a beautiful, healthy baby girl. Please come back and show her off."

"I will! Thank you so much."

In Jason's office, Michael asked about Malaika's transportation home. Jason assured him that Alicia, his Program Director who was helping Malaika, would take care of that. "It's what we do here—help out in small ways, and when we can, make miracles, so those with very little can get their basic needs met."

> "Too often we underestimate the power of a touch, a smile, a kind word, a listening ear, an honest compliment, or the smallest act of caring, all of which have the potential to turn a life around."
>
> *Leo Buscaglia*

"Do you think Malaika's homeless?"

"I don't know. Alicia will talk with her. We don't require our clients to confide in us but if they choose, we help them where they're at. Given that she's held a job for a year, my guess is that she has a place to stay. But she's eating a lot of McDonald's food and the month lasts longer than her money. She may be staying at her boyfriend's place or couch surfing with friends. Hopefully she's able to come back to see one of our counselors. Then we can connect her with social services to keep her and her baby healthy, as well as build trust with her. Then if an event in her fragile life takes a turn for the worse, this will prevent her becoming homeless with an infant."

"I hope Malaika comes back, Jason," says Michael, sighing deeply. "She obviously works hard but doesn't make a living wage. She's focused on providing for her unborn child, yet she has so little that she needs to come 10 miles across town to get a few baby clothes. How many are there like her?"

"The statistics are daunting. Most young people we see don't have jobs, can't find jobs, can't hold jobs, or don't want jobs. We work with them from where they are. We hope to get them into more stable housing and help them build a foundation for their lives to get those basic needs met. The alternative is chronic homelessness, poor health care, survival sex, legal hassles—it's bad."

"Thanks for coming to the office, Michael. This place doesn't compare to the digs you're used to, but it's home to us."

"What's important is the work you do. That's why I'm here."

"Thanks. And yes, we deliver services, as well as find transitional shelter for our homeless youth that have aged out of foster care or run away from a bad home environment."

"I'm looking forward to hearing more about your plans for NextPlace4Good. I retired from my company, but not from life. I've been reading about 'encore' careers and 're-wirement,' looking for the right opportunity. After four-and-a-half months of this, my wife is equally interested in me being involved and engaged again in meaningful work."

Jason had been preoccupied all afternoon, concerned about how he could continue to make payroll. After watching Michael's response to meeting Malaika and hearing about this retired businessman's interest in exploring what's next for him, Jason felt reinvigorated. He put on his game face and said, "Let me give you the fifteen cent tour and then we can talk."

Jason guides Michael into a lengthy corridor. "This building is owned by another nonprofit that provides counseling services. They moved into a new building and rent this space to us below the market rate. It's the first time we've had a place of our own where we can provide services to homeless youth. We get young people immediate help. Then, if they're ready, we work with them on their life skills, their high school GED, and job opportunities that get them on a track of independence. Without our assistance, more times than not, the alternative is prison—or worse."

At the first opening in the corridor, Jason extends his arm to open a door. Michael enters a classroom with a computer at each desk. "This is where we work one-on-one with our clients. We evaluate their reading and math skills, which are almost always very low. For example, we just evaluated Justin, age seventeen. His parents couldn't handle that he is gay. After a year of essentially being expelled from his family, he ran away. Unlike many of our clients who have been in foster care, Justin has had decent school attendance, reads only a little behind his grade level and can handle basic algebra. He's an excellent candidate for taking the GED, and he has a foundation of life skills we can build on to help him develop independence."

They walk down the corridor to a larger room with small offices. "These are social worker offices where clients receive both counseling and services to help them get off the streets. Being homeless is awful for anyone, but young people are especially vulnerable on the streets. They are physically and sexually assaulted, robbed of what little they have and life is a downward spiral from there."

"How are you able to help?" Michael asks. "And do you find them— or do they find you? I guess I'm also wondering how many times you're successful and what you know about the impact you're having on these young people's lives?"

"We have some great success stories. When we have a real turnaround like Moses Wilson, for example, we know we've made a difference. Moses aged out of foster care without being taught the life skills that your own children got from living in your house. Moses was bouncing around from one friend's couch to another friend's car to wherever. Our outreach van found him and encouraged him to come to our day center. Eventually, he came and started to show up regularly to shower, wash his clothes and talk to a counselor. When his trust in us was high enough, he signed up for our transitional housing. You might think young people living on the street would jump right away at hot showers, free food and lodging. But the housing we provide also requires something of them because we impose a lot of structure on their living circumstances. Most street kids aren't ready for those imposed structures right away."

"What kind of structure are you talking about?"

"The residents share an apartment that comes with specific chores. They must be dressed and in the dining hall by 8:00 a.m., be out working or studying until 4:00 p.m., be at dinner at 5:30 p.m., finish evening chores by 7:00 p.m., lights out at 10:00 p.m. They receive the equivalent of gold stars that entitle them to TV and video games when they conform. They run the risk of their room being given to others when they break house rules."

Michael was glad to hear that NextPlace4Good provided structure, rewards and consequences for young people living and benefiting from the services this nonprofit organization provides.

"Moses is an example of someone who liked the structure and that caught the attention of our counseling staff right away," explained Jason. "This young man worked diligently toward getting his GED and was accepted into the freshman class at Arizona State University. He needed orthodontia, so the local dental foundation is now arranging for him to get the dental care and braces he needs. Moses will start classes this fall with a new self-confidence, a scholarship through our fundraising, and a savings account of his earnings we have been keeping for him while he's been growing up in our housing. We need more stories like Moses."

Michael could see that Moses was certainly an encouraging example of what's possible when homeless youth receive a supportive environment and the assistance they need.

"To answer your question about who we're helping and how we're impacting their lives," Jason explained, "last year we served 315 homeless youth. Twelve young people earned their GED certificates—our best ever annual result. Forty-one landed a job and moved into supportive housing. We opened up bank accounts on their behalf, taught them about banks, and taught them how to save money. We loaned these youth the security deposits for their apartments, phones, utilities, etc. Unfortunately, we've lost track of 114 clients who either moved on to another city or just simply stopped coming. Our remaining clients are engaged with us to some extent. We celebrate the successes, but the statistics are not as great as we envision, especially considering the published statistics on homeless youth are likely very understated. Our typical client avoids shelters, is distrustful of adults, and is less visible."

Jason decided honesty was the best policy at this point in his discussion. After what seemed like a very long pause he continued, "You might have joined a sinking ship Michael. I hate to be a pessimist, but it's going to get worse, I'm afraid. Our charitable donations are 36 percent below several years ago after the shock of the Great Recession. Government funding no longer covers the cost of our services. I don't see a way right now to deliver the same level of service in the coming year as we did last year. It's a shame to start our relationship off on such negative news, but I think you should hear it sooner rather than later. The cities and towns in the Greater Phoenix Valley of the Sun have all reduced funding for social services dramatically. Look at this article about our local communities."

Jason showed Michael a newspaper clipping. He skimmed through the highlighted sections.

"While some Valley cities have cut back on funding for non-profit agencies because of budget constraints, a conservative faction on the Gilbert (AZ) Town Council wants to do so for philosophical reasons.

The discussion has sparked concern among non-profits that already are dealing with higher demand and sagging revenue in a tough economy.

Gilbert has slashed the amount it gives to non-profit agencies like food banks and homeless shelters by about 40 percent since fiscal 2009, but some on the council want greater cuts. . .

. . ."To take one person's property only to make it someone else's property is not appropriate. . ."

. . . Other municipalities, including Scottsdale, Chandler and Surprise have also cut back on non-profit aid, but for different reasons. Scottsdale this year reduced its general-fund allocation from $200,000 to $100,000, a move that was "strictly a financial decision based on less revenue available in the general fund for everything..."

. . .The cuts included a 54 percent reduction in funding for Central Arizona Shelter Services, which operates three homeless shelters in Phoenix that serve about 10,000 people from across the Valley...

. . . Representatives of local charities contend they are providing services that benefit the entire community. . . "We have to continue to help our neighbors."

*by **Parker Leavitt***

The Arizona Republic

Michael rubbed his chin thoughtfully. "I guess the only thing I can say without really knowing the answer is this: I will work with you to figure out how to survive and then grow from there. Many times during my business career I had to face seemingly insurmountable problems, including financing, but I never gave up. Somehow my team and I developed answers and the problems got solved. We moved ahead. I know we can do the same here Jason. I really do."

"It's getting late. Why don't we grab a beer and you can tell me more. Okay?"

"Sure thing. There's a tavern around the block that's a good place to talk."

In the booth at the Village Tavern Michael asked, "I'm curious about you, Jason. Where are you from? I see you're married by your ring. Do you have any kids yourself?"

"Well," Jason said, as he took a sip of his beer, "The short answer is that I grew up in Chicago, graduated with a Bachelor's in Psychology and a Master's degree in Social Work from the University of Illinois. I went to work as a counselor for the Cook County Employee Assistance Program. I met my wife, Polly, at a party while we were both living near Lincoln Park. She also grew up in suburban Chicago and went downstate for college, but we didn't know each other in Champaign. She graduated with a degree in Accounting, has a CPA, and works for Deloitte in their audit group. We got married in Chicago five years ago."

Michael interrupted, "It sounds like you knew counseling and nonprofit work were going to be your career. Was there a compelling reason that led you to work in this field and at NextPlace4Good?"

"Actually, I don't think about it too often now, but in high school I took a community college psychology course, and it was my best course in high school. Besides learning about psychology, I also learned about myself. It was the first time I had thought about who *I* was and what kind of person I wanted to be. I went for the Master's degree more for the credential and more job opportunities."

"And to answer your original question, Michael, my wife Polly is pregnant now with our first baby—due in April."

'That's wonderful! Having a baby will be a gigantic change in your life, but you'll love it!"

"That's what everyone says. We're looking forward to it. After our second winter together in Chicago, we decided to move to a warmer climate. She was able to arrange a transfer to Phoenix, and I quit my job. An opening for a counselor at NextPlace4Good became available. I applied and got hired. So that's how I ended up here."

After Happy Hour ended at 7:00 p.m., Michael called his wife, Jackie, and Jason called his wife, Polly, to say they'd be home late. Both husbands wanted to continue their conversation over dinner. Jason felt Michael's genuine interest and was hopeful he had a partner in the mission of NextPlace4Good: "A Safe Shelter for All Kids." Michael, too, felt optimistic that he had found the opportunity to make a difference in his community during his retirement.

Over dinner, Jason filled Michael in on more details about NextPlace4Good. "Last year, Peggy Brooks, CEO of the organization since the beginning, retired. The board conducted a big external search. They hired and relocated a replacement CEO from Pennsylvania who had worked with kids. After five months he quit—just like that. All the effort and expense went down the tubes. Joe just wasn't a good fit for the organization, and neither he, nor his family, liked living in Phoenix. Six months ago, the board figured it would be lower risk to promote from within. I was in the right place at the right time and got promoted. The board said that I have leadership potential, I know the organization, and they are willing to give me a coach or a mentor so I can 'grow into the position' so to speak."

Michael concurred. "I agree with them. Curt asked me to join the board for that very reason."

"Well, what they didn't expect, Michael, was this downturn of fortunes in our financials. I have growing confidence in my ability to manage the people and the work. I'm even decent at the fundraising. But I've never had to deal with the degree of revenue shortfalls that could destroy the place. I have to develop my board presentation to explain the financial reality, and I'm not sure what to recommend. It looks to me like NextPlace4Good will need to cut back so drastically that we won't have enough staff. Our future viability is in real question."

Michael had been listening closely to Jason's story. Michael had served on a number of nonprofit boards throughout his business career. He valued serving on boards because it helped him develop business, but more important to him, he viewed board membership as a way to contribute to his community. As a retired executive, Michael now saw that he could choose the social cause of his passion and not be tied to the strings of his business. His close friend Curt, current chair of the NextPlace4Good board of directors, encouraged Michael's participation on this board. The more he learned, the more excited he became about the opportunity. Serving homeless youth became the social cause of his choosing. To Michael, providing life skills, transitional housing and job training to those without their own resources meant turning around a human life. He could see that his own life experience and recent thinking about what could be the "encore" to his successful business career had prepared him well to empower NextPlace4Good to fulfill on their mission in a big way.

> "When you're using your business acumen to help people struggling with mental illness, get homeless youth off the street, or work with abused kids...you may go home frustrated over work...But you never go home wondering why you went to work in the first place; that's front and center all the time."
>
> *Jim McClurg,*
>
> *Social Enterprise Alliance*

After several audible deep breaths, Michael finally responded. "Jason, I hear you, and I appreciate your candor and honesty with me after we just met a few hours ago. I'd sure like to start out in a stable and growing environment, but I understand that's not where we are. Will you indulge me for a moment? I have a few questions that may seem off the subject."

Jason nodded.

"Okay, when we were back in your office you said NextPlace4Good had served 315 homeless youth last year. How many homeless youth are there in the Phoenix area? Of all the organizations that provide services, how many or what per cent are being served in some way?"

"Well, in rough numbers, one other large nonprofit in Phoenix with a mission similar to ours serves about 1,000 homeless youth. Other shelter organizations around the Valley might serve another few hundred or so youth. That means, in total, we serve roughly 2,000 homeless youth. As you might expect, an accurate census of who needs help isn't readily available. Homeless youth avoid shelters and any places with authority, so they're especially not counted accurately. National statistics for our size metropolitan area with a mild climate, probably has a population approaching 20,000. That could be the reality Michael—20,000 homeless youth passing through Phoenix during a year."

"Jason, you're joking."

"I wish. It turns out that too many kids raised in foster homes don't get the attention and parenting you think. Then, when they age out of foster care at age eighteen, poor life skills, no high school diploma, one disruptive incident and they find themselves on the street. One-third to one-half of them experience homelessness within two years."

"Good grief. I had no idea."

"There are other reasons a young person might end up homeless in Phoenix. Kids who haven't reached their 18th birthday often run away from a bad home environment—abuse, alcoholism, drugs, gangs. And the likely outcome for homeless young people is that they end up committing a crime, get caught, and are then put behind bars."

"So you're telling me that only ten percent of the young people who need our services to get housing, jobs and the skills to be independent adults receive services, either from us or another agency in our community? *Ten percent*? Did I get that right?"

"That's what I'm saying. It's a shameful situation, but that's the reality. And as I was telling you, I don't see how we can even deliver services next year to the same number as we did this year. That's how bad it is."

"Wow. While I don't mean to short change the importance of NextPlace4Good's financial straits, I needed to understand the vital role our nonprofit organization plays in the community. Jason, we must find a path to succeed in the short term because we need to solve the large scale problem in the long term. I'm hoping you'll accept my offer to help in whatever way I'm able. I'm the eternal optimist, and in my business life, I've always met big challenges by not giving up. My business results so far have been pretty good. In fact, one of my staff members called me a 'Solutioner' because I keep looking for the path to success. By being tenacious and never giving up, other folks around join me because they know I'm seriously committed."

"Thanks, Michael! Of course, I accept your offer." With Michael's partnership, Jason was feeling more and more positive, although presently, nothing had really changed.

"Your optimism is contagious," exclaimed Jason. "I was feeling pretty worried this afternoon. Thank you for stepping up to make a real contribution!"

"No thanks necessary, Jason. I consider this first financial instability a challenge for us to beat, so we can move on to the real task at hand— causing a bigger positive impact on our community's homeless youth. I like the saying. 'Never let a good crisis go to waste.' Let's figure out how to use this difficult financial situation to our advantage."

In his own mind, Michael was already considering possible first steps, but he knew they were both tired.

"You never let a serious crisis go to waste. And what I mean by that, it's an opportunity to do things you think you could not do before."

Rahm Emanuel, former
White House Chief of Staff for
President Obama

"Now it's time for you to go home to your wife, Polly, and for me to go home to mine, so I can tell her I'll be fully engaged with NextPlace4Good. Jackie will welcome the news because she informed me last week she married me for better or worse—but not for lunch! I've been around the house only four-and-a-half months, but, according to her, it's been four months too long. Remember that, when you get to my position. Good night Jason and I'll call you tomorrow to come in and get a better look at our dire straits."

"Good night Michael. And thank you again. I look forward to working with you and benefitting from your financial insight and wisdom."

"I don't know about the wisdom part Jason, but I do have a wealth of experience that should come in handy."

The Crisis

Jason spent the next two days pulling together all the information Michael had requested: their strategic plan, which hadn't been updated during the last year of turmoil; last year's budget; the income and expenses of this year to date; IRS Form 990s for the past few years; data on the employees; statistics about their clients and any grants the organization had received.

Jason didn't usually close himself off for hours on end in his office and not interact with staff and clients. Curious, his Program Director, Alicia Adams, interrupted him on the second day to ask what was going on.

"Our newest board member, Michael Collins, a retired businessman, has asked me to pull together materials so he can understand our organization from a business perspective. We should have these materials together for ourselves, so I'm using his request as a good reason to get our financial act together."

What he didn't mention to Alicia was the neglected state of what the documents and numbers actually revealed. As he studied the monthly financials that the accounting firm had been giving him, Jason saw the erosion in revenues over time. The organization hit its peak revenue of $1.5 million two years earlier and would likely only reach $1.1 million in the current fiscal year.

Michael had asked for a Profit & Loss statement, a balance sheet and a statement of cash flows. Jason hoped he would be satisfied with the budget report that listed programs, fund development and administrative expenses, along with a list of income sources. Jason realized he had not really looked at the out-of-date strategic plan goals since his first week as CEO, when he thought he had the breathing room to implement those goals. Now when he looked at the aspirations of growing fifteen percent in revenues and developing new collaborative relationships, it felt like he was reading about some other nonprofit. Nothing in the goals seemed remotely possible at the moment.

Michael came by late Thursday afternoon to pick up the material. Jason handed him an organized binder with tabs for the strategic plan, the last two year IRS Form 990s, this year's budget detail, and a hastily assembled schedule of income from donations, grants, business and government support. He also included a section with NextPlace4Good annual reports and marketing collateral.

"It's not exactly what you asked for Michael, but I was surprised that it took me the better part of two days to lay my hands on the material, and I hope you can make sense of it. Fundamentally, two years ago we had a surplus of $300,000 when our revenues were $1.5 million. If we achieve $1.1 million of revenues this fiscal year, the surplus of $300,000 becomes a deficit of $100,000. That would eat into the Net Assets of $342,000 we've carefully built since our founding twelve years ago."

"Jason, I get the picture. Typically I've taken the first ninety days of any new assignment to immerse myself in understanding the organization. Based on our conversation earlier this week, I'd better get going because ninety minutes, not ninety days will be too long."

Michael left with the understanding that as soon as he was able to digest the material, he would call Jason to discuss the immediate future needs.

Then he drove to his home office in Scottsdale to spread out the notebook papers and review the information.

Soon, Michael had his laptop open and was setting up some templates to assemble the data he had been given into a form more meaningful to him. From the 990s, he could see NextPlace4Good was eating into its Net Assets for about $100,000. The precipitous drop in contributions and business support, combined with increases in expenses like employee health care, was partially offset by a grant from a local family foundation. But the situation was tenuous with no obvious solution in sight. Michael studied where all the income sources had been over the past two years. The expenses were trimmed. Almost three-fourths of costs were salaries and salary related. That left little room for cost reductions, since the electricity, phones and basic purchases were the only remaining expenses. Michael recast the numbers, so it was easier for him to explain. Then he called Jason and said, "I'm ready to talk when you are."

They set up a Saturday morning breakfast, the start of a habit for them. They met early at the local Butterfield's since the weekend crowd gathered there about nine. Jason was anxious to hear Michael's thoughts after reading the material. He hoped Michael was still optimistic.

"But what if he isn't," thought Jason. "What if Michael doesn't see a path to get out of the red ink?" Jason decided to put this fleeting thought aside while waiting for Michael to order breakfast. Coffee and an omelet for Michael, fresh squeezed orange juice and pancakes for Jason.

Finally ready to begin the meeting, Michael said, "Here's the thing, Jason. In order to take action, we first need to be grounded in the reality of the situation. That means we've got to get a good grasp of the numbers and what they are telling us."

Jason's appetite vanished. "So you don't see a way out either?"

"I didn't say that," Michael continued. "I will admit, what I read was not a pretty picture, and I don't have an instant answer that will solve all our problems. But we have to discuss the future with a clear, grounded understanding of where we are and what we need to do about it."

Jason calmed down a bit.

"So," said Michael. "I'm going to ask you some questions that will require you to think before you answer. Don't say the first thing that comes to mind because you won't have thought through the implications. This year's revenues from all sources are less than expenses by $100,000. What are the programs and activities that you can stop doing that will save us that amount of money?"

"There isn't anything that would save that much," Jason exclaimed. "I guess we're hosed!"

"Now you're just reacting, which is what I'm asking you *not* to do," Michael smiled

"Let's think about it. We need to explore every avenue of expenses, then every avenue of short term revenues—and give ourselves some room to breathe, that is, to *plan* for a more sustainable financial and programmatic future. And we can't do that until we solve our immediate sustainability problem."

Jason and Michael talked back and forth for almost two hours, ordering more coffee and orange juice. They promised the waitress a big tip for letting them sit and work. They came up with several ideas for reducing expenses. For example, Adam Rosen, the athletic and social activities counselor at NextPlace4Good, had wanted to go back to school. Although Jason didn't like the idea because he preferred to keep Adam on full-time, he agreed with Michael that the organization could offer Adam a part time position, meet his educational goals, and save the organization more than $20,000 of expense.

Another cost savings they formulated would be to share the GED classroom training space with another local nonprofit that helped women re-enter the community after being released from prison That cost sharing would potentially reduce an additional $15,000 of expense. After Michael and

Jason added the bits and pieces of savings actions, they moved to revenue enhancements. By the end of the work session, they had identified nine actions that could yield an annual net of $100,000 and rebuild the diminishing cash account.

"Jason, if I hadn't walked through the door, what were you going to present to the board next week?" Michael asked.

"That's exactly what I was struggling with right before our meeting last week. I knew we had a financial problem, but I still didn't have any solutions to recommend" Jason admitted. "I've been working my butt off, building relationships with staff, donors, clients and board members. I've watched over the expenses, and I've earned a reputation with my staff as a skinflint and a miser. In fact, they nicknamed me 'pencil-boy' because they think I count when they take a pen or pencil out of the supply cabinet. But it's really because I know we're in dire straits, and haven't had a better solution."

With Michael's assistance, Jason felt relieved and empowered, even though he also felt a bit guilty. "I thought I was handling the budget, but I hadn't developed a get-well plan like we just did. It will be a lot of work to turn around our financial situation, but now that it's down on paper, I can see the path to achieve our financial goal and deliver on our mission."

"Great, Jason! That makes me feel like I can be of value, not only in the present, but also for the future of this valuable organization. Here's what I want you to do now. Take our list of nine items and develop an Action Log. List each item in the log, assign the item to the proper person, even if it's a board member, and agree with that person on the completion date and the person accountable. You and I will review the Action Log progress each week. Will these Saturday morning breakfasts work for you?"

"Saturday breakfast is good. That's when Polly goes to the gym, so it's good. I'm thinking I want to present the Action Log at the board meeting."

"That would be a good as *part* of the presentation, Jason," said Michael, "but based on my discussions with Curt, it's not clear how much the board really understands the organization's current financial status. You'll need to explain that first, but the good news is that showing the Action Log will build their confidence as well."

"Will do, Michael. Thanks for the help. And thanks for picking up the breakfast check!"

The Action Log

The board meeting was well attended. Curt Applegate, board chair and executive at the local electric utility, had called each member and informed them that this would be an important meeting and urged them to attend. Jason summarized the financial statements and forecast at the outset of the session.

After giving them the difficult news, Jason spoke with confidence to the somewhat unnerved board members who had not realized the severity of the revenue shortfall. "And this is our Action Log, which we monitor each week."

Pointing towards his Program Director, Jason said, "Alicia Adams has responsibility to follow up on many of the expense items. I have responsibility for the revenue actions."

"Why are we just now hearing this?" asked one concerned board member. Other board members questions and body language indicated they, too, did not like being surprised with negative financial news, a lesson for young Jason.

Michael intervened, explaining that the deterioration had happened gradually and that the board must recognize how fortunate it was that Jason had identified the situation so early in his tenure as CEO. Michael's explanation and Jason's presentation of the Action Log eventually eased the tension in the room. Although they didn't like to admit it, board members also realized that the negative financial report reflected poorly on them for not being more attentive to their fiduciary responsibility.

NextPlace4Good
ACTION LOG: For Review January 23*

<u>Goal:</u> $100,000 annual improvement in Profit and Loss Statement achieved within 60 days through a combination of expense reduction and additional revenue.

Date Assigned	Action with Expected Results	Assigned To	Complete Date	Complete YES/NO	Impact Estimate	Impact Actual	Comment
1/16	Move Adam to part time position	Adams	2/15	YES	$ 24,500	$24,500	Salary + benefits
1/16	Rent computer room to others	Adams	~~3/15~~ REV: 4/15	NO	$ 15,000		Will meet revised date

* Completed Action Log chart in Part 2

1/16	Renegotiate lease	Greene	3/15	NO	$ 10,000		Might be $8,000
1/16	Employee vs. company paid holiday party	Adams	1/16	YES	$ 2,500	$2,500	Budget reduction
				TOTALS	$100,000	$52,500	

Michael spoke to his fellow board members as a "newbie" but someone who has served on other charitable boards. He was prepared to keep them uncomfortable even further.

"Fellow board members," he said. "What we've just discussed is only a short term financial fix that's intended to provide us the time to develop a sustainable financial future for NextPlace4Good. Recently, I met a young man—a client at the facility. I'm sure he's typical of the young people we serve. He's bright and personable, but what would happen to him without us? He left home in California because of his abusive father. He's lived with friends here but couldn't figure out how to get into school. He found our program; we helped him get a job and a shared apartment. Eventually, we helped him get financial aid to attend community college. He told me his father had never taught him about money. Now he's accumulated $1,200 in savings! He had no concept of how to earn money, save money, use money to rent an apartment, or buy a car, and the list goes on."

"What will happen to young people like him without us? Many will predictably be robbed of what little they have, start shoplifting for basic necessities, get caught and go to prison—never, ever learning the life skills that NextPlace4Good can teach them."

Michael continued, "That's just not acceptable to any of us! We will have to focus full time for the next two months on the "Action Log" items. That is our current path to survive. But we need to work together with Jason to develop a *sustainable* future for NextPlace4Good."

"And one other point that needs to be made while we're in a serious discussion," Michael added, "our purpose, on behalf of the Phoenix area community is to assist homeless youth to become independent, employed and in a safe shelter. Right now we're doing that for about two percent of the young adults who need our services. Including *all* other organizations like us in the Phoenix area, collectively, we still only serve ten percent of the people who need our services! While we take pride every time we assist a homeless youth in getting off the streets, serving only ten percent means that as a group of nonprofits, we are all collectively failing the community."

"In my business life I would have said when all providers together have captured ten percent of an available market, there's a wide open market for our services. But even *more* pertinent is our responsibility to the community that has granted us tax exempt status. How do we intend to meet their expectations by realizing our mission?"

Curt Applegate now stepped in and addressed the entire board.

"As you all know, I asked Michael to join our board because he has the energy, and now the time, to help us well-intentioned, but busy folks make NextPlace4Good successful. And he has already helped Jason organize our short term actions. When Michael and Jason explained the situation to me in preparing for the board meeting, it became obvious we needed both a short term action plan and a longer term strategic approach. Developing these short term plans and long term strategies will require us to really think through our future goals. I'd like to start the discussion in 60 days, giving us a chance to make progress with the Action Log tasks, but still keeping the discussion on our front burner. I'm asking you to clear your calendars for Friday, March 16 and Saturday, March 17. I'll work with Jason and Michael to develop the agenda for the meeting."

Michael interrupted Curt, "What would you think about bringing someone from the outside to facilitate the session? That way all of us could be active participants, and it's been my experience that a consultant helps the session stay on track, accomplish the meeting goals, and enable each person to have his or her say."

Curt spoke for the board, "Well, hiring a consultant is an expense just at the time we're cutting expenses to the bone. I do understand your point, and it's also been my experience that good consultant facilitators deliver more value than their cost. But let's add a tenth and eleventh item to the Action Log then. We can engage someone, but we also have an action to cover the consultant's costs."

"Got it, Curt," Michael agreed. "I actually have someone in mind that I've worked with before. Her area of expertise is social enterprise, that is earned income opportunities, but she's a strategic thinker and would be a huge help in organizing and facilitating the session we're talking about. I think if the relationship works out, she can help us beyond the meeting facilitation. This first meeting will be a good test of the chemistry between her and us."

Ask Why 5 Times Before Asking How

The next sixty days were a beehive of activity. Michael met with Curt, Jason and Alicia on a weekly basis to review progress on the Action Log. The cost actions were quickly put in place and it appeared that savings would slightly exceed the estimates developed. The revenue items were coming along more slowly, and it looked like the hoped for donors and small grants to cover existing programs might not reach the goals. That's where Michael focused more of his attention, probing and asking, "Why?" Then, after Jason answered, Michael would ask again and again, "Why? Why?"

"We have commitments for $9,000 from repeat annual donors versus a goal of $20,000," Jason reported.

"How have we reached out to these annual donors in the last thirty days?" Michael asked.

"We've sent this letter and then followed up with a phone call."

Why?"

"Well, other donors typically write us a check in December as they do their tax planning."

"Why?"

"What do you mean Michael?" Jason thought his answer was obvious.

"I want you to keep answering the *why* questions so that you think more deeply about the situation, as well as think more deeply about other approaches and solutions. For example, if donors have been including us in their annual contributions for several years, what we do must be important to them. Whereas I don't know the exact way to engage them now—in the middle of the year, I believe we can develop an approach based on your understanding of what we mean to them, why they give to us, and how else we might reach out to them. This problem solving technique is called 'Ask Why 5 Times.' The technique's proven to get to root-cause problem solving where most solutions deal with symptoms."

So Jason continued answering Michael's "why" questions, like "Why do people give to this organization?"

"They give because we tell stories about the young people we have helped and how they then help themselves. Donors relate to us because our clients are like their kids."

"Why?"

"Because they know kids who became drug users or high school dropouts and haven't had the benefits their kids have had. They see us as a way to reach those kids whose parents haven't done the job they have. We're like surrogate parents."

> "People give to you because you MEET needs, not because you HAVE needs."
>
> *Kay Sprinkel Grace,*
> *Author and fundraising professional*

"Okay Jason, now I think we have the makings of an approach. That resonates with me as well. It's exactly the reason I feel strongly about working with NextPlace4Good. Let's map out a relationship building strategy, including working with our board members to ask key donors to increase their support to these youth."

Meet the Team

Michael had met Sarah Stoneham while he was on the board of the Boys and Girls Clubs of Arizona. She was able to effectively shepherd the thirty-person board to develop meaningful multi-year goals and get widespread agreement between board and staff members. Each board member felt he or she had gotten the opportunity to participate and be heard. Individual staff members were equally positive about their involvement.

Sarah was an M.B.A. and had considerable private sector work experience before she shifted her career to social purpose organizations. She felt strongly that the nonprofit sector had dedicated leaders and workers. But for all their hard work, she could see that missions were not being accomplished. She had dedicated this next part of her career to identifying ways to enable leaders and boards to achieve the missions of their organizations.

Michael invited Sarah to the next Saturday Butterfield's breakfast with Jason. She summarized her background for Jason's benefit, but mostly, she listened as he and Michael talked about NextPlace4Good. She listened to the details of the short term action plan and their vision of a sustainable, yet high growth future.

As they ate and talked, Jason envisioned the steep hill they were asking themselves to climb. In addition to being overwhelmed, he was feeling exhausted at the thought of more sixty day sprints in his life as a CEO. With the baby due any day now, he wanted to step away and have more personal time. Maybe he should ask for his old job back and let them hire a new CEO. But then, would his old job be there if they didn't find a way to become sustainable? Was he as trapped as he felt?

Sarah interrupted his spiraling negative thoughts. "After listening to you, Jason and Michael, here's what I think we might do. Let me know what you think."

She paused, "We have to look at the big picture first before we select our course of action. You say the strategic plan is outdated. It also sounds like a business as usual, incremental improvement philosophy. The Great Recession has taken the business as usual option away for nonprofits. To develop our new business model, we'll first take a look at some macro indicators, perhaps looking at trends in youth homelessness, in funding, in the local economy and the like. I suggest looking at some other organizations to learn what they've done, how they've handled the economic downturn and benchmark ourselves against them. This is work we can and should do in advance of the workshop. It will give us a foundation of knowledge to share with the board and senior staff who will attend. I assume your staff will attend. Correct, Jason?"

"I hadn't thought about it. We've been consumed with our short term recovery. But yes, they have a lot to contribute and should participate in whatever we discuss. I'll select the right folks and invite them."

"Great. Then, if you want, I can start researching the trends. But it would be good to work with you, get some sources, get your input on interpreting what I discover and then summarize it for publishing to the attendees about ten days before the meeting."

"I can help also, Sarah," Michael offered. "I've been working with Jason and can take some of the load off him with preparing material. I can keep him informed and up to date, but his plate is really, really full right now with top priority things. Oh, and he's about to become a father for the first time!"

"Wow!" Sarah exclaimed. "That's wonderful, Jason! When is the baby due?"

"Well, you notice I've kept my phone on the table during our whole breakfast, just in case I get a call," Jason smiled. "The official due date is in two weeks, but my wife, Polly, has been having contractions pretty regularly now and her doctor says I should stay close. It's a girl, and she might pop out any time now."

"That is so exciting!" Sarah exclaimed. "Given you must be a bit distracted by your daughter's imminent arrival, I'll work with Michael on getting the research done and then we'll meet with you to get your input. What I think is most important during the workshop is for the board and senior staff to discuss how the trends affect NextPlace4Good and to develop a SWOT analysis and then. . . ."

"A *what* analysis?" Jason asked.

"Sorry, it's spelled S.W.O.T. It lists the most important Strengths, Weaknesses, Opportunities and Threats for any organization. The Strengths and Weaknesses are largely from an internal focus and the Opportunities and Threats are external to the organization. The analysis fulfills two important objectives. First, it gets everyone on the same page. When the board and staff haven't met together, having all stakeholders aligned on the strengths, weaknesses, opportunities, and threats regarding their organization is important in and of itself. Board members also typically bring a perspective from their business and professional life, while staff members are well grounded in what's happening out in the real world and in the organization. Combining board and staff members' perspective has proven valuable."

Sarah continued, "The other value of the analysis is as a springboard for the discussion of multi-year strategic goals. There can only be a few of these, and they have to be the most important goals. They become the guiding direction for the annual objectives you as the CEO and your staff and board will follow. Although they aren't cast in stone, strategic goals provide the best knowledge of how to fulfill the mission, and they are not changed without considerable debate. Strategic goals are developed leveraging the Strengths of the organization and the Opportunities available, while keeping Weaknesses and Threats in an organization's peripheral vision. Does that make sense?"

"Yes, thanks," Jason replied. "I think I had heard of this type of tool before, but I haven't done a SWOT analysis and didn't catch the acronym when you first said it."

"Good, so then a positive outcome of the two-day workshop," Sarah continued, "would be to develop a very few, but important multi-year goals that would give direction. Three goals would be sufficient. Five goals would be an absolute maximum. For an organization the size of NextPlace4Good, five is really too much. I would rather develop three or four strategic goals at the max."

"Can you put together an agenda reflecting that flow, Sarah?" Michael asked. "We would want to review it with Curt, but it really sounds on target for where we are."

"Absolutely, Michael. And thanks for picking up the breakfast check!"

Setting Strategic Goals

For the strategic goal-setting meeting, Jason brought three staff members: Alicia, the Program Director; Adam, now working part-time but knowledgeable about the organization; and Deb, their Office Manager/Bookkeeper. Eight of the organization's nine board members could attend both days of the workshop. These members included Howard, an attorney at a local law firm; Kathy, a CPA with a Big 4 firm; Curt, who, in addition to being board president, was also an executive with the local power utility; Michael, now spending an average of twenty-five to thirty hours a week with NextPlace4Good; Betty, a nursing supervisor at one of the hospitals owned by a national hospital corporation; Darren, a young, high talent manager at a semiconductor fabrication plant; Julia, a community volunteer and wife of a college baseball coach; and Matt, manager at a local professional job placement agency. Chuck, a psychologist who worked with teenagers and young adults, had previously committed to a family vacation and was unable to make the session.

Sarah began the day of strategic planning with a roundtable discussion of each person's expectations, which she wrote and posted on flip chart paper. Then she reviewed the two-day agenda, clarifying the purpose of each topic. She linked each board member's expectation noted on the flip chart to the agenda topic where that expectation would be discussed and, hopefully, met.

Then Jason presented an update of the Action Log. They had closed the large gap between expenses and revenues, with only an $8,000 gap remaining. Jason and his team received a round of applause from the grateful board members.

Sarah linked the progress of the short term recovery to the urgent need to develop a sustainability plan that was longer term focused. She reviewed the agenda, clarified the purpose of each topic, and answered questions about the deliverable output of each topic.

Michael, Sarah and Jason took the leadership to present their findings on environmental trends. Key trends they identified included the following:

TOPIC	RELEVANT TRENDS*
The Economy	◆ The Phoenix area economy has reached bottom but is recovering very slowly compared to cities in other parts of the country. ◆ The record high historical population growth of the Phoenix area is slowing. Projected annual growth rate for the next decade 2.0% - 2.6%. ◆ Joblessness is also worse in Phoenix than other cities, greatly affecting the lower skilled labor base. Arizona is ranked 2nd in the nation for job growth before the great recession. Arizona's rank descended to 49th during the recession as the combination of construction, retail, semiconductor, tourism and retirement losses eliminated 1 job in 11. ◆ The job recovery will extend slowly over many years.
Homelessness	◆ Homelessness overall has taken a turn for the worse because of housing foreclosures; family homelessness is a potential impact for NextPlace4Good as homeless children become teens.
Tax Exempt (nonprofits)	◆ Collective Impact of many organizations being deployed to solve difficult issues. ◆ Partnerships and alliances considered as a minimum ◆ Alliance of AZ recent nonprofit survey: "Borderline: Hope and Concern for Arizona Nonprofits." Findings include: About 45 percent of nonprofits will have to reduce their budgets . . . and nearly 30 percent expect to end. . . (current year) with a deficit. Revenue losses are moderating. The mean decrease in nonprofit revenue is 16 percent. . . down from 18 percent in (previous year) and 22 percent in (the year before that). . . ."

* Completed trend analysis in Part 2.

Board and staff members discussed trends until late morning. The need for services is growing, and the sources of secure funding are shrinking. No wonder they had a gap in their budget. Sarah intervened as the discussion took on a tone of helplessness.

"Let's take pride that, as the board and staff, you have now proactively dealt with a serious financial deficit during turbulent economic times. Take heart in your accomplishments. They have given us the chance to develop a stronger, more sustainable future and to better perform our critical community mission. I have confidence that, over the next two days, we will lay out a path to meet our needs."

After the lunch break, Sarah moved to the next topic. "We chose to benchmark organizations that could either teach us or inspire us, or both, as we develop the strategies for the future. The first organization we chose is Teach for America, founded in 1990 by a twenty-one-year-old college graduate, Wendy Kopp. She saw inequity in educational opportunities determined by where a child was born. Based on Wendy's long term vision, as well as developing and executing on a strategic plan, Wendy built a global organization to address inequity. Let's look at what Teach for America has achieved. But more importantly, let's examine some of the processes they developed that benefited their organization, and thus, benefited children."

Sarah's Summary of Teach for America's history

High Growth – Tax Exempt (Nonprofit)

Teach for America (TFA)
www.teachforamerica.org

"One day, all children in this nation will have the opportunity to attain an excellent education."

Inspirational Vision

Founded 1990, Wendy Kopp, age 21, based on Princeton undergraduate thesis. Raised $2.5 million on challenge grant from Ross Perot and hired 500 corps members in 6 communities. Important milestones. . .

2000 – 10 anniversary	Launch of aggressive 5-year expansion campaign to double corps members from 1,500 to 3,000 and to 30 communities by 2005. *5-Year Strategic Plan*
2005 – 15 anniversary	3,500 corps members, and 22 communities.
2007	Launch of *Teach for All* to spread model to other countries.
2010 – 20 anniversary	Has 8,200 corps members in 39 communities and 20,000 alumni corps members

Teach for America   Page 2 of 2

Four Priorities

4 Priorities with goals & measurements

1. Grow in scale and diversity – in 2010, 10% growth in corps members; 12% of all seniors at Ivy League colleges apply; 1 in 4 African American seniors and 1 in 5 Latino seniors apply.
2. Maximize the impact of corps members on student achievement – 2010 Univ. of North Carolina Portal Report; 2009 Urban Institute study; 2008 Calder Research Center. Internal measures: Corps members who effect significant gain 53%; solid or significant gains 77%.
3. Foster the leadership of our alumni as a force for change – measured by alumni in school leadership; political leadership and as social entrepreneurs; 25% increase in FY2010.
4. Build an enduring American institution – financial sustainability goals for Teach for America. Revenue Sources (2009 IRS 990): Contributions and grants 90%, Program Service Revenues 8.5%, other 1.5%.

Sustainability Model?

Sarah walked the attendees through her summary, highlighting those processes that she believed contributed to the extraordinary growth and success of Teach for America. The five-year planning horizon with measurable annual progress was the hallmark of a great management team and board.

Despite the high growth, tremendous attitude change, and the best practice planning processes that Teach for America had accomplished, Sarah also pointed out that its revenue sources were still highly dependent on contributions and government contracts. In other words, the earned income portion of the organization had grown to only a modest percentage of total revenue.

> "We have the problem of educational inequity not because children in low income communities and children of color aren't motivated or can't do the work, not because their parents don't care . . . but because we as a society have not given them the opportunity they deserve. **We can solve that. And if we can . . . then we must.**"
>
> *Wendy Kopp, Teach for America & Teach for All*
>
> *2009 Skoll Foundation Award for Social Entrepreneurship*

"So we can learn and admire Teach for America," said Sarah, "and we can also see where they now might want to focus their efforts to earn additional revenue in support of a great organization with a valuable mission."

Sarah was happy she could see board and staff members start getting interested in alternative sources of revenue, even for a successful organization.

"Let's now turn to a social purpose organization, one that is young, but with a financially sustainable business model. I learned about Better World Books from a book club member. She had ordered a used book online, but instead of the usual shipping notice to her email, my friend's 'book' had written her a very cute 'thank you for buying me and getting me off the dusty shelf' email!"

Sarah thought this "book's" email message was such a clever and unusual shipping notification that she did more research on the organization that wrote and delivered it. She learned that three Notre Dame University graduates with post-graduation blues launched Better World Books in 2002. "Of course," said Sarah, "I now frequently order used books from *Better World*. But I also follow their progress as a for-profit social purpose enterprise."

"To date, we have raised millions of dollars for literacy, saved millions of books from landfills, created jobs for hundreds of people, and provided wonderful books to millions of readers worldwide. The rest of the story is still being written. We invite you to join us on our journey. It's only going to get better."

Excerpt from www.betterworldbooks.com

Sarah continued, "They began collecting old textbooks that the bookstore wouldn't take back and sold them via an online book exchange. The initial sale was so successful that it gave these three social entrepreneurs the idea to build their own online textbook exchange. Here's a brief history from their website."

Triple bottom line for profit "B Corp"
<u>Better World Books</u>
www.betterworldbooks.com

Certified Benefit Corporation

"Teach the world to read."

Inspirational Vision

"Tired of seeing all the piles of old textbooks sitting around the apartment, they tried a hunch and put roommate's old books for sale on the Internet. The campus bookstore never paid much for used books. Buying and selling stuff on the Internet hadn't gone mainstream yet. They became intrigued by the online book market, and wondered how to find a lot more books . . .

Encouraged by the success of the book drive, the new partners decided to draft a business plan. They recruited their friend and classmate from the world of investment banking to help build the business. They envisioned a different kind of company with a built-in social benefit. By generating revenue to fund literacy, they would also earn profits to support and grow the company. And in funding literacy, they would help give struggling people the world over the skills and self-esteem necessary to thrive and succeed.

The three founders submitted the idea to a Notre Dame University business plan competition, and won "Best Social Venture." With $7,000 in prize money and some guidance by a competition judge who would later become CEO of the company, the entrepreneurs then set off to run Book Drives for Better Lives on campuses across the country.

Business Plan Competition

The environment becomes a stakeholder too . . . every year thousands of libraries had millions of excess books as they made room for new editions. Some books sat in storage, and others were given away. But some were simply thrown out. Tossed. Abandoned to the landfills for all eternity.

Convinced that something could be done to rescue these discarded books and help the planet a bit in the process, the founders set about partnering with librarians all across the country. Not only could they rescue books from landfills, they could also sell those books and raise money for the libraries themselves.

Library's Social Enterprise

Environmental *and* social impact all in the same story."

This would be no ordinary business. The founders examined all the standard business practices anew, and they considered the impact of their business on everyone involved. Not only would they harness the power of commerce in a socially and environmentally beneficial way, but they would also create an organization with a conscientious, forward thinking culture where innovation, creativity and humanitarianism would thrive.

Well, they did.

And they called it Better World Books.

Triple bottom line – profit, people, and environment

Sarah asked the group, "What is it we can learn from Teach for America and Better World Books?"

Julia spoke first, "Both vision statements give me goose bumps! They are compelling, clear, confident. Of course, so is "A Safe Shelter for All Kids"!

Curt was sitting back in his chair. "These are good organizations, but why didn't you select a homeless youth nonprofit to benchmark?"

"Great question, Curt. It's because there are different kinds of benchmarking. For this exercise, we are doing *strategic* benchmarking, trying to expand our thinking and horizons by studying the strategic success of others. As an example, if we wanted to expand our scope and market, we might study how Coca-Cola moved from seeing themselves as a cola-soda company to deciding they were in the beverage business, then expanding into bottled water, orange juice, etc. I picked these two different organizations where they have some especially strong attributes we can discuss. Not in this group certainly, but in some other sessions, a group might see an example close to what they do, and find reasons to dismiss a best practice because the organization is too big or too small, or has a different history. It might be a distraction from seeing the right attributes."

Sarah continued, "But I would add that when we want to do operational or financial benchmarking like cost per hour of service, or percent of clients that get a GED, then we should look at how we compare to similar organizations. Does that make sense?"

> "Strategic benchmarking involves observing how others compete. This type is not industry specific, meaning it is best to look at other industries."
>
> *Wikipedia – Benchmarking*

"Yes, thanks, Sarah. I'd like to do operational benchmarking also when we can."

The discussion continued. "Both organizations seem to be widely known and publicized," suggested Darren. "At least by comparison with us."

"Teach for America has changed the way we think and behave," offered Betty. "When I graduated from college, new teachers looked for jobs in the suburbs to avoid inner city schools, and certainly, graduates with degrees other than teaching didn't apply for teaching positions. TFA created a *movement* that attracts some of the best new graduates in all disciplines!"

"It's interesting how Teach for America has developed a series of five-year plans and measured their progress to each goal," said Alicia. "I think that would benefit us a great deal."

"A comment on Better World Books" Michael added. "They have a sophisticated business model that serves their compelling mission statement as Julia said earlier. And as a B Corp they have also harnessed the profit motive. I respect Teach for America, but the earned income of

Better World Books from book sales is much more sustainable than the ten percent or so Teach for America program service revenues. And we could benefit a great deal from that predictability."

Sarah called for a break before the next session. "We are now ready to develop our own analysis. We will be combining our *collective knowledge* of NextPlace4Good with the *trend research* we presented. We'll leverage those *benchmarked attributes* of Teach for America and Better World Books we just highlighted. Next we will complete the Strengths, Weaknesses, Opportunities and Threats or SWOT Analysis using one flip chart page for each. Then I will summarize our ideas."

NextPlace4Good SWOT Analysis*

Strengths	Weaknesses
• Staff and management dedication • Staff and management competence • Track record of results and success stories	• Financial (in-) security • Overworked staff
Opportunities	Threats
• "Un-captured Market" of 18,000 homeless youth in area • "Alumni" base as supporters • Job training, skill-building and job creation for working age homeless youth • Earned Income from business that employs homeless youth – some clients currently earn "stipends" for work at supportive housing	• Government budget deficits restrain funding • Recession causing more homeless youth

* Completed SWOT analysis in Part 2

After the meeting, everyone adjourned for cocktails and appetizers. Sarah observed the tone of the conversations. It seemed like the attendees were much more upbeat than at lunchtime. Hearing about others' successes— and experiencing their own success as they developed the SWOT analysis strengths and opportunities—gave people a "can do" boost. Sarah thought, let everyone "sleep on it" and then tackle the most important topic in the morning.

The next day Sarah introduced the idea of goals and objectives—terms that are often used to define each other. "We're going to assign specific definitions to the terms 'goals' and 'objectives' so that as a team, we speak the same language."

"When we say 'goals,' we will refer to statements of multi-year strategic importance. We will limit goals to no more than four for the entire organization, so these are our main aspirations. 'Objectives' will support each of these goals; they will be defined and measured on an annual basis and will be reported to the board as part of a 'balanced scorecard' at each meeting. Objectives will be specific, measurable, agreed to, realistic and time-based—in short, SMART. The objectives will come later. For now, let's discuss the goals."

With that foundation, Sarah worked with attendees to develop four multi-year goals:

NextPlace4Good Strategic Goals

Goal 1: Develop inviting and welcoming methods to bring homeless youth into NextPlace4Good programs.

> **Measurement:** 15% annual improvement on client feedback report.

Goal 2: Create or join an ecosystem of organizations that support homeless youth to independence in all necessary ways: economic, behavioral, psychological, educational, vocational, social and life skills.

> **Measurement:** Develop ecosystem and have joint written goals with each ecosystem partner.

Goal 3: Develop a business that both trains and employs our clients while earning income for them and for NextPlace4Good. Use this as an opportunity to expand our horizons and better fulfill our mission.

Measurement: Implement a profitable workforce development social enterprise within the next 18 months.

Goal 4: Develop a predictable donation income by nurturing the relationship with our donor base and engaging them in our work and results.

Measurement: Quarterly progress updates to board and 15% annual increases.

Isabella – 7 lbs. 2 oz.

After the meeting, Jason was emotionally exhausted. At the same time, he saw a future for the organization. The retreat discussions made him conscious of the board's passion for the mission and how much support they offered to him and the staff. He wasn't sure how he would develop the objectives that support the goals, but he had hopes that Michael, and now Sarah, would help him rise to the challenge.

He and Polly went to their favorite Mexican restaurant to celebrate. Polly kept adjusting herself in the booth, but she was happy to be with Jason for an uninterrupted evening together. "Jason," she laughed, "the nurse told me that having spicy food was a sure way to start labor. Wouldn't it be a stitch if this burrito did the trick?"

Wouldn't you know, at midnight Polly woke Jason. "Honey, my water broke! Time to go to the hospital."

Polly's contractions were still modest, so Jason took a quick shower to wake up while trying to remember all the calls he would need to make in the morning. He scribbled the list on a piece of scrap paper, stuck it in his pocket, and then concentrated on his role as a birthing coach.

Jason was a great coach, helping Polly along the way, until he became unnerved seeing her struggle. As the baby's head emerged, he couldn't contain his excitement and tears. Polly's doctor handed him the most beautiful baby girl with instructions to walk her to the exam table. His daughter was looking wide-eyed at her father. Jason was sure she knew him.

After changing from hospital gown back into street clothes, Jason found the call list in his shirt pocket. After the initial family calls, Jason called Alicia, covering all the necessary open items so he could take the next week off. Alicia promised she would call if anything major came up. Jason asked her to email the notes of the meeting as soon as they were ready.

He hadn't been this happy or exhausted ever, but his beautiful baby girl, happy wife and successful workshop renewed his optimism for all things.

Do We Have Consensus?

Michael called Sarah for a post workshop review to discuss what might be next. They met for breakfast and each brought their notes and thoughts. Sarah worried, "I hate to have this conversation without Jason."

Michael concurred, "I would prefer he be here also, but he needs this time to be with his family, and he's earned the time away. I wanted to talk with you while the meeting was still fresh in our minds. I will take notes and review everything with Jason. What we can do to help him is develop an approach so the next time we meet with him, we have a 'straw horse' for discussion. Sarah, why don't you start? What were your feelings about the workshop?"

"I thought we accomplished a lot. I thought some of the background material came as a surprise to most board members and perhaps some of the senior staff as well. I believe everyone got over the shock and participated in the discussion in a positive, problem solving way. Well, almost everyone. I thought Howard was a bit reluctant to agree with all the multi-year goals we set. I'm not sure what he was thinking, but I felt he wasn't completely on board with all the ideas. Did you think so, too?"

"Good summary, and yes, I sensed a reticence from Howard, especially about the goal to explore a business venture that could employ our clients. I'm not sure what was behind it, or how strong his opinions are. On the other hand, when we discussed our possible business venture, I noticed definite enthusiasm from Curt and Darren. Oh, and while I'm thinking of it, I need to set up a separate meeting with Chuck, who missed the whole session. I can bring him up to speed. I also want to take advantage of his professional psychology background and hear his comments. He'll be an important board member as we work toward these goals."

Michael continued, "Despite what may be concerns from Howard or others, I thought we accomplished what we needed to. We now have the foundation to develop our next year's objectives and that should primarily be Jason's work effort with us as reviewers. I want to focus with you on two of our goals: creating a business venture and developing a network or ecosystem of involved organizations. That's where I see that I can add the highest value. And now, having worked with you, Sarah, that's also where I think you bring skills the organization needs."

"I'm thinking along the same wavelength Michael," Sarah said, smiling and nodding. "That's why the SWOT analysis will become very important. We'll build off our strengths and leverage the opportunities that the team listed."

Michael suggested Sarah work up a retainer agreement with NextPlace4Good. He asked if she would back-end load her fees so that the start-up funding for the social enterprise would be available to cover some of her expenses for the business planning. She agreed to prepare the agreement for review and to estimate the scope of what her work effort might be.

"The first thing I'd like you to research," Michael asked, "is a list of the kinds of social enterprises other communities have that employ our type of client: young and strong, not well educated, able to be trained, coached and better educated. The list needs to be consistent with the environmental trends you researched and the SWOT we developed. This list, along with some examples to make it real, will focus our discussions. We can get to the market needs and network opportunities later."

"That sounds like a good approach," Sarah agreed. "My schedule frees up later this week. I can get started on both the research and the retainer agreement then."

"Excellent," Michael responded. "If I get any brainy ideas during the week, I'll shoot you an email."

SECTION 2:
A Social Enterprise – But What?

So Many Choices . . . Pick Me!

When Sarah returned to her office, she drafted a retainer agreement that was back-end loaded. NextPlace4Good would pay a portion of her fee on a monthly basis. About half would be deferred until the organization obtained some initial funding. This wasn't her preferred consulting arrangement, but then, most projects had some quirks.

As she wrote the agreement, Sarah thought about the number of pro bono professional services made available in the community. She had also given much her personal experience and time for free. After all, many nonprofits had no cash on hand to pay her, but what a false economy.

It sounds attractive. One of her consulting colleagues observed, "Free advice is worth what you pay for it." Sarah agreed. In a mission critical project, no matter how passionate the professional, in the end, pro bono work is less important than fee-based projects. And when the recipient organization has no skin in the game, it does not place a high priority on its resources being involved. The pro bono talent might have great expertise, but how elusive it is to capture that value. The end result—lots of excuses and apologies. Projects stay in limbo, when they should already be finished and on the path to achieving their desired outcome. Getting a solid foundation under a social enterprise is a mission-critical project.

Once her agreement was drafted, Sarah researched successful examples. She was able to identify several U.S. cities with clusters of social enterprises that employ those with barriers to employment. San Francisco, Seattle, Chicago and New York each had well documented examples. The businesses employed the homeless, disabled, re-entering the workforce, in recovery, youth at risk, or aged.

These model nonprofit organizations provided the infrastructure, business skills, training and ongoing management for people who are potentially difficult to employ. The types of businesses included:

- Janitorial services for commercial buildings
- Bakeries that sell retail and wholesale
- Landscaping and lawn maintenance
- Assembly or subassembly as a contract manufacturer
- Basic work, like making pizza boxes or shredding documents
- Laundry and dry cleaning
- Restaurants and coffee shops
- Community gardens
- Art galleries
- Repair work on HVAC units, appliances, electronics

Sarah wondered how NextPlace4Good should think about their options. "What would I do if I were Jason?" she thought. As Sarah reviewed NextPlace4Good's SWOT analysis alongside her researched list of nonprofit organizations using alternative employment methods, she also browsed several websites of social enterprises before jotting down her own prioritized list.

Most relevant to NextPlace4Good:
- Commercial janitorial services
- Landscaping and lawn maintenance – commercial buildings
- Community gardens
- Art gallery/craft sales

Other possible businesses, requiring more upfront capital investment:
- Bakeries
- Restaurants

- Coffee houses
- Laundry and dry cleaning

Not a good fit
- Basic assembly work - might fit more physically or mentally disabled populations and would not produce the income needed for either the employees or the organization.

After categorizing the options, Sarah wondered if there would ever be an opportunity to extend into more skilled business areas, like air conditioning repair or computer repair. Would there be an opportunity to develop a low-cost product design and actually own the intellectual property, as well as income, from manufacturing and selling the product?

When Jason returned to work, the three social enterprise thinkers met. After hugs and congratulations, Michael and Sarah asked to see pictures, asking Jason how it felt to be a new dad.

"I'm 32 years old, educated, double income family," said Jason. "I look at Isabella as she's sleeping and think, what must I do to insure that she's given the life skills to live independently and never find herself a client of NextPlace4Good? I feel the responsibility, as well as an enormous contentment, nervousness and happiness—all mixed together!"

Michael and Sarah nodded in agreement, both having raised their children, remembering the early days as a first-time parent. Then they got down to business.

Sarah first explained her consulting approach and recommended billing schedule. Jason was intimidated by the cost of getting to the business plan, which didn't even include the startup costs of whatever they chose. Sarah pointed out (and Michael concurred) that what they were doing would be a real business. And just like any business, there was risk associated with it. The business planning process provides a way to think through the approach, reducing and avoiding risk. Given the importance of the organization to the community, business planning is the only responsible way to launch a new venture and not put the nonprofit organization itself at risk.

"An ounce of prevention is worth a pound of cure," Michael offered. "In my career, when the appropriate attention has not been paid up front, the cost of fixing mistakes is often 10 times or 100 times the cost of preventing those mistakes in the first place. Not all of them will be avoided, but hopefully, the serious errors can be prevented."

Additionally, Sarah pointed out, other than volunteer board members, who certainly do their part, the skills required to plan and launch the business were not ones that currently existed within the paid staff of the organization. They were skills that Sarah brought through her experiences both in the corporate world and with other nonprofit organizations.

"So here is what you get when you engage me as consultant:

- Your project gets a schedule and stays on schedule.
- You get the benefit of my real life experience in business, as well as drawing on the expertise of others. My experience also tells me when we have enough knowledge to take action.
- My business planning methodology—particularly my knowledge of what is important, what questions to answer, and how to view a marketplace where people have choices about how to spend their money.
- Overall risk reduction—for failure or falling short of the goal.
- A document that will make sense to any potential investor.
- An approximate discount of 50% over the same advice given to a for-profit organization."

"So the way I see it," said Sarah, "your primary concern after you validate my references should be the following: Are you comfortable working with me? If so, then why would you *not* hire me?" After discussing the decision a bit more, all three shook hands and agreed to proceed. Sarah showed Michael and Jason the raw list she had compiled of social enterprises employing the difficult to employ, providing a real example of each one from her research.

Social Enterprises
Employing the Difficult to Employ

"A Safe Haven" – Chicago, IL, offers supportive housing and addiction treatment, then life skills, job training and employment through its multiple social enterprises, including landscape services, catering, pest control, housekeeping and food services.

"Boston HandyWorks" – Boston, MA, building maintenance and repair, apartment turnover, weatherization services; training and employing homeless, supervised by skilled staff.

"Roberts Enterprise Development Fund (REDF)" – San Francisco, CA, a portfolio of selected organizations for which REDF offers a combination of funding and business assistance over several years. "Investing in Employment and Hope." Portfolio includes organizations that operate a wide variety of social enterprises that train and hire the difficult to employ.

"Growing Power" – Milwaukee, WI and Chicago, IL, "hands-on training, on-the-ground demonstration, outreach and technical assistance through the development of Community Food Systems that help people grow, process, market and distribute food in a sustainable manner."

"Greyston Bakery" – Yonkers, NY, supportive employment producing upscale restaurant desserts and brownies for Ben & Jerry's ice cream. "We don't hire people to bake brownies. We bake brownies to hire people."

"ReliaTech" – Greater Metropolitan San Francisco, CA, provides technical training and workforce development in low income communities, creating high paying jobs to support and maintain computers and networks for small business, nonprofits and individuals.

"Toolworks" – San Francisco, CA, a janitorial business with a ten-week training program for homeless and other low-income individuals with disabilities.

"Goodwill Industries of Central Arizona" – Phoenix, AZ, "We put people to work." The mission is to serve people with disabilities or people who would otherwise face obstacles to entering the workforce. In 2011, more than 35,000 people received services at Goodwill and 12,481 were placed in competitive employment.

"How do we select from the list?" Jason asked, after they had covered all of the options and examples. "It feels like we could do any of them and all of them!"

Michael responded, "Perhaps someday we will have multiple businesses, but for now, it's important to select a single one for two critical reasons. First, we need to understand the market need for *any* product or service we would offer. Just having a workforce won't bring sales in the door. That will be our first and most important task, once we make our selection. Second, we hardly have the time or financial resources we need now to do a single business, much less consider multiple options."

Sarah suggested they use a point system to do an initial ranking: award points based on the Strengths and Opportunities from the SWOT, points when one of the options requires less startup capital, points when the option is expected to earn higher revenues, and points when the option appears to better train clients for future independence.

"Let's assume we have 100 points," Michael offered, "and then split them according to the rankings Sarah has suggested. Are there any other categories we should add?"

Jason was absorbing the list, intently focused on the options. "Should there be points where we intuitively think there's a higher market need?" he asked. "I can see, for example, lots of lawn care services, but not nearly as many wonderful bakeries in town, especially in certain neighborhoods called 'food deserts,' where, according to the USDA, 'there are limited retail outlets selling healthy and affordable foods.'"

"Good catch, Jason!" said Sarah. "That would be an excellent addition."

After their initial brainstorming, Sarah, Jason and Michael developed a matrix with each criterion assigned maximum points based on its particular importance. They made sure the total points for all criteria added up to 100.

Criteria	Maximum Points
Fits Strengths of NextPlace4Good and its clients	20
Identified as Opportunity in SWOT	10
Lower Start Up Capital Required	15
Expected to earn high revenues	15
Expected to better prepare clients for future jobs	25
Expected Higher Market Need	15
TOTAL POINTS	**100**

They discussed the distribution of points. This process highlighted the importance they placed on the business having a dual purpose or "double bottom line" of preparing their clients as part of a workforce. Sarah suggested they each assign the points individually. Then the next time they met, they could develop a consensus on the options.

As planned, during their next meeting, Michael, Jason and Sarah brought their completed scoring sheets. They went opportunity by opportunity discussing their thinking and where their scores differed. Mostly they were in agreement, although Jason had some clear preferences and biases. The other two deferred to his judgment on what would be suitable. They selected a consensus score for each criterion of each opportunity. The basic assembly and capital-intensive opportunities received the low scores of 35-40 points out of a possible 100. The team agreed that work was probably not good training or good employment to encourage further education by their clients.

Community gardens and appliance/HVAC repair got the highest scores at 75 and 80 points out of a possible 100. These became the two opportunities to explore further.

NextPlace4Good – Opportunity Analysis*

Opportunity	Fits SWOT Strengths	Fits SWOT Opportunities	Low $ Start up	High $ Rev. Potential	Work Training of Clients	High Market Need	TOTAL
Points	0-20	0-10	0-15	0-15	0-25	0-15	0-100
Commercial buildings janitorial services **	15	10	10	5	10	0	50

*Complete Opportunity Analysis in Part 2.

Laundry and dry cleaning	5	5	5	5	10	5	35
Restaurants and coffee shops	5	5	0	5	15	5	35
Community gardens	20	10	10	10	20	10	80
Repair work on HVAC units, appliances, electronics	10	10	5	15	25	10	75

**NextPlace4Good could leverage existing use of clients who work in supportive housing units.

As a way to narrow the field of play to a single opportunity, they made a list of people to speak to and collect more information. Curt was high on their list. In fact, he had been calling all three of them on a regular basis to get updates. Additionally, they put Howard on the list to identify his concerns and bring them to the team to discuss. Among the three of them, they were able to identify folks in town who would be knowledgeable about a successful business model for either the garden concept or the appliance repair concept.

Each of them took an assignment and drafted the questions they wanted answered before the meeting ended.

Jason's research on appliance repair quickly pointed out the need for repair people to have both driver's licenses and vehicles to get to appointments. The training and licensing (to work with Freon) would be highly valuable to clients; however, training courses to send individuals out by themselves could take more than a year. He found a wealth of information at the federal government Department of Labor website. His research notched the opportunity a peg lower because of the time involved in building a sustainable business.

Jason's research on the community garden concept led to discussions with other nonprofit leaders about holding Farmer's Markets in areas of the city where fresh vegetables and fruit weren't easy to buy in the neighborhood. The areas are known as "food deserts" because the choice of fresh food is limited, isn't particularly fresh and is high priced. Other nonprofits have supported community gardens by and for the residents in the area, but the concept of a social business had not been pursued in Phoenix as it had in other cities like Chicago, Milwaukee and the San Francisco bay area.

Jason's enthusiasm grew. When he met with Michael and Sarah, he laid out his game plan.

"Here's my idea. We work with the city and get free use of vacant city-owned land where we can set up parking, awnings for shade, an entertainment area, food court area, etc. We use our clients as staff for the Farmer's Market and to tend an urban garden where we sell our produce, as well as charge for tables for other farmers. We also get rent from concession booths for food, kettle corn, etc. We do this in one of the identified food deserts and sell our produce below supermarket prices. Perhaps we can get a supermarket chain to support us and sell produce at cost to help us fill in what we don't or can't grow. We can also launch new products, like honey or cheese that we make ourselves! What do you guys think? Don't you think it could be great?"

Michael whistled. "Wow, Jason, I guess you have been busy in those night hours when Isabella wakes you up. That's a real mouthful of ideas. I think part of the success equation is really being invested in the business, and it sounds like as our CEO, you find this exciting. That's important in itself."

Sarah, also surprised by the new, energized version of Jason, also chimed in. "Wow is right! We started with lists and analytical tools, all of which helped us as a team talk about our opinions and learn more about the reality. And you've taken this idea and developed it in your own mind's eye so that it's already happening. How entrepreneurial Jason. I love it."

"Yeah, I guess I got carried away." Jason was embarrassed that he had taken such a strong stance.

"No, no don't misunderstand," both Michael and Sarah said at the same time. "It's a *good* thing that you're excited about your idea! You just surprised us."

"Well, I do think it's a great fit for us. Our office is in the neighborhood where a Farmer's Market would work, there are many in Scottsdale or higher income areas around town, but none here where they are needed. Also, the other markets charge so much for renting tables that buying produce there is twice as expensive as going to the supermarket," Jason continued.

"What do we do next?" he asked.

Sarah stepped in. "Let's write down our idea so we can talk about it and get it shaped up. When we're happy with it then we'll bring it to the board. Assuming it makes sense to proceed, which I would imagine it would, we would begin our analysis of the Market Opportunity just as we would if we were a for-profit enterprise. I use a series of questions that help us research and decide what the needs are, what people will pay for, and exactly where in the entire space of the market will we focus."

Michael added, "While you do the write up, Jason and I must meet with Howard to understand his concerns."

"Okay then. It's Melons to Money for us!" Sarah announced. What I mean is we are launching a new enterprise—a market-based way of thinking about our revenue streams as part of fulfilling our mission. We're going to grow and sell melons! And peppers and kale!"

They all laughed and enjoyed the joke.

Yes! We Have Consensus

"Thanks for meeting with us, Howard," Jason began. "We brought our strategic goals with us today. It seemed like you had reservations about the goals we established at our workshop. We want to understand your thinking, specifically about our earned income initiative, which seems to us like a possible lifesaver."

Michael added. "Yes, Howard, thanks for seeing us. We've continued to work on the concept of earned income, and we'd like to share our thoughts with you, but why don't you start the conversation and share your thinking. We value your experience and want to incorporate all the knowledge of our board."

Howard sat back in his office chair and looked at the ceiling for a moment. "I guess it all boils down to a concern about mission creep. Right now we're focused on the young men and women who are homeless—helping them recover their lives with programs that heal, teach and support them as they work toward independence. It seems that working on something other than the focus on these youth takes our eye off the ball. That's my concern."

Michael responded, "Yes, Howard. And it's our responsibility as board members to make sure we stay on mission. So your concern is valid. I come at it a slightly different way. When I joined the board only four months ago, Jason was explaining how the organization would probably need to reduce or eliminate services based on funding shortfalls. That's when we launched the short-term survival plan, which, thanks to the great staff at NextPlace4Good, has closed the gap between income and expenses. So we'll be able to keep services flat or level with the prior year. Great, but as Jason explained, even with all organizations combined, our organization and others like us are really only serving a small, small percentage of the youth that need our services. So in my mind, the question is *how can we say we are achieving our mission unless we are able to expand services to youth who need those services?"*

Jason interrupted, "Michael's right, Howard. When you look at Maricopa County and the large number of homeless youth, we're not doing the job we need to do. And I can tell you that we won't be able to accomplish our mission by relying on grants and government funding. Perhaps we can find a high net worth individual who will fund us, but short of that, we need to develop a sustainable funding model in order to expand."

"Jason, are you telling me you can do both with the resources you have? That's where I doubt it. You're already working long hours and so is everyone else there."

"I am telling you I can do both. I can say that because Michael has been spending a great deal of time helping me. He has also brought on Sarah to the team. She brings the framework for the process that I don't have and helps me see how it can be done. Otherwise you're right. I couldn't do both, and I wouldn't see how we could rise above this quagmire."

"Howard, we have been working great as a team. Jason brings incredible insight into the situation. He is also quite energized by the possibilities we've been analyzing. And as he mentioned, Sarah brings the process knowledge that we need, plus more business experience and brain power to apply to the situation."

"I have another agenda item, which is this: I would like to ask you to help us also. As part of our discussions with Curt, he is going to appoint an ad hoc committee of the board to oversee our work. The committee will engage board members with relevant backgrounds so we get the benefit of their professional expertise, as well as oversight. Of course, your legal expertise is important on this committee, so Curt will be asking you to be a committee member. I would like you to consider chairing the committee. In addition to the legal expertise you would add, I greatly value that you spoke your mind and your concerns. We don't want people who just accept what we say. We want people to challenge actions they don't agree with and do it in the constructive manner that you have just done. Would you consider becoming the Chair?"

"You flatter me, Michael," chuckled Howard, "which I assume is meant to get me to take on the role of Chairperson. Well, it actually does interest me to be involved in the ad hoc committee as you called it. I can probably Chair it as well. You have such a way with words!"

Everyone laughed and shook hands on it.

Game Plan Brief

Sarah, Jason and Michael developed a concise briefing paper that could be sent with the regular board package. They asked Curt as board chair and Howard as ad hoc committee chair to read it in advance.

Jason and Michael met with Curt and reviewed the brief. Curt liked the idea but was concerned about the ability to pull it off.

"What if it doesn't work?" Curt asked. "We've just spent ninety days working to keep the doors open. It's not like we're flush with money or time."

"Good point, Curt," Michael agreed, in order to add the obvious. "While we don't know if it will succeed, if we don't try, then we'll be in the same crisis mode every year. This is an idea that we believe delivers a more predictable revenue stream, while at the same time, provides a direct mission benefit. We're suggesting taking the steps to develop the idea into a robust business plan. If we can do that, we will be improving the likelihood of pulling it off."

"I see," Curt replied reluctantly. "While what you say makes sense, it still feels a lot like a shot in the dark with an organization that's really needed by a lot of people. As board president, I have to be conscious of our governance responsibilities."

NextPlace4Good
Social Enterprise Briefing Paper
Farmer's Market
April

Strategic Goal #3: Develop a business that both trains and employs our clients while earning income for them and for NextPlace4Good. Use this as an opportunity to expand our horizons and better fulfill our mission.

> **Measurement**: Implement a profitable workforce development social enterprise within the next 18 months.

Background: This brief is intended for a social enterprise idea that benefits clients of NextPlace4Good, low income communities and the NextPlace4Good organization. This idea was chosen among an extensive list of opportunities that matched the strengths of our organization.

Requested Action: Approval to proceed with a business plan that will either confirm the idea or help us select another alternative for the strategic goal.

The Idea: Identify vacant, preferably city-owned land with adequate parking. Identify another close-by plot of land with water that can be developed into an urban garden. Employ the clients of NextPlace4Good to clear the two sites, one as a Farmer's Market, one as a garden. Local small farmers and ranchers would be able to sell their goods at a reasonable price. The location would be in a so-called "food desert" where low income residents, many without cars, must travel outside of their neighborhood to shop for fresh, affordable food.

Train and employ our clients and provide them with secure bank accounts to save their earnings. NextPlace4Good earns rental income from the Farmer's Market, as well as from selling produce grown by us.

Start-up funding may be syndicated from a variety of sources to be determined.

NextPlace4Good
Social Enterprise Briefing Paper
Farmer's Market
April

Estimated start-up expenses (rough): $50,000 - $100,000

Risks: (1) Dependability of client workforce, (2) ability of crops to grow and be sold, (3) renting fewer spaces, (4) fewer buyers. There are a number of successful examples to study and learn from to reduce our risk.

Skills: A business plan consultant, Sarah Stoneham, to facilitate the research and draft a written business plan in concert with Jason and Michael.

An ad hoc committee of the board to oversee the work and meet with the team every 60 days; four to five members, each with a different set of professional skills.

A master gardener / urban garden expert in both set up and operations, including a Farmer's Market. Initially can be a part-time position growing to a full-time position with the growth of the social enterprise.

Approximate Schedule: 1-Year Elapsed Time

Approval to proceed	May 1
Market Opportunity Analysis	May - June
Business Plan Development	June - August
Board Business Plan Review & Approval	Sept - October
Acquire start up financing	Oct – Feb
Hire key personnel	Feb - March
Business start-up – garden, marketing, agreements	April
Opening Day	May 1

"Understood Curt. Jason, Sarah and I are going to think this through very carefully, and as you have read, we're asking the board to monitor our work as we go. We met with Howard because of his reservations when we identified a social enterprise strategic goal. Not only did he accept becoming a member of the ad hoc committee, but with only a bit of encouragement, he has also agreed to Chair the committee. His thoughtfulness and thoroughness will keep us all grounded. Jason is fitting this into an already long workday in order to create a brighter future for the organization and its clients. So you have our commitment to be prudent."

"Amen to that," Jason offered. "I will continue to monitor the daily operations, the action log and work through this business planning. Now I'm feeling like we haven't engaged Sarah enough for all the work we have to do on the business side."

"Sarah is already heavily invested in making this a success," Michael suggested. "I'm sure if we give her enough notice on her schedule, she will make herself available to us."

"I'm starting to feel that overwhelmed feeling again," Jason replied. "I'm thinking about giving her some office space, so we can work more closely together on this."

"Great idea, Jason," both Curt and Michael concurred.

Curt said he would email them his nominees for the ad hoc committee of the board.

Board Committee on Board

Over the course of the next two weeks before the scheduled board meeting, Jason and Michael called or met with each of the board members to explain in advance what they had been working on and what the discussion would entail at the board meeting. They emailed the document during the call or presented it if they met in person. They reviewed the brief and engaged each board member in a give-and-take discussion. The social enterprise concept was foreign to most board members, so they spent considerable time discussing and explaining their social enterprise idea with each board member. They also used the examples Sarah researched as indications that Social Enterprises were gaining momentum and could be developed by managing risks with good market analysis and thorough business planning.

Curt provided them the list of potential ad hoc committee members. After initially briefing a nominee for the ad hoc committee, they asked whether that person would also serve in an oversight manner. All agreed they would, perhaps without really understanding their role.

The ad hoc committee included the following members:
> Howard, attorney and Committee Chair
> Kathy, CPA
> Darren, marketing
> Julia, community leader
> Chuck, psychologist

The board meeting agenda had only two items: (1) an update on the short-term Action Log status of survival level funding, and (2) a review of the Social Enterprise briefing document.

Jason and Alicia covered the Action Log Update. All items had been acted upon with good success and the $100,000 gap had been almost completely closed. The $4,000 that remained and the $8,000 upfront business plan consulting payment to Sarah needed further work. Toward that end, Jason and Alicia had come prepared with a new action to raise the final $12,000 through one of several local foundation opportunities. This Action Log process was now familiar to the board, so the board was now able to consider more strategic and sustainable financing options.

Curt introduced the briefing document topic and talked about his discussion with Jason and Michael. Sarah had also joined the meeting at this point. The three organizers moved to the front of the room.

Jason spoke: "Thank you all for discussing this with us prior to the meeting. We value your input and the time you spend contributing to our critical mission. During our March retreat, we developed our strategic goals. After that, it became my responsibility, supported by Michael and Sarah, to analyze our options and develop how we would make those goals a reality." Jason paused.

"What we have shared is our process to date. We've looked at multiple options and developed a weighted ranking of each option in the attachment. The option we have selected as our number one choice is the option that I personally see as a huge win-win for the organization and the community. Today we are asking for board approval to proceed with spending the time and resources to develop the business plan. I can go into considerable detail about why I feel strongly that a Farmer's Market and Urban Garden are perfect for us, but I know from our discussions that you are keenly interested in what happens next and how we go from an idea to a real business plan. That is the expertise that Sarah brings to us, so I will ask her to lead the discussion now. Sarah?"

"Thanks, Jason." Sarah stood to speak. "Many of you may have been presented with business plans as part of your work life. Perhaps you have even written business plans. I have seen lots of them, in lots of formats, and even software packages that guide a planner through the process." Sarah watched as several board members listened with interest about what she would share next about writing and executing on business plans.

"As a result of preparing or reviewing lots of business plans, I have organized the process to be coherent and purposeful. There are two primary benefits of documenting a business plan. The first is to get all players on the same page. Even in a rare situation where a single entrepreneur is building his or her own business, an effective plan serves to clarify ideas and necessary actions. In almost all cases, more than one person is involved in the planning process. This provides the setting for a team of key players to contribute value, to agree or disagree, to achieve consensus, and, by doing so, work toward common achievements."

"The second benefit of the process," Sarah explained, "is to reduce risk inherent in any business enterprise. By clearly targeting a segment of the market and understanding that target market's needs, their buying behavior, and specific ways to reach them as customers, we are able to focus our scarce resources in ways that maximize success and minimize risk. Additionally, by examining all aspects of our business in a disciplined fashion, we are able to identify gaps and fill them as we launch. As part of this disciplined process, we specifically think about risks and develop plans to mitigate those risks."

Sarah paused to allow board members to consider all of what she had just explained before they asked questions or made comments. "Before I go further, do you have any questions?"

Betty raised her hand. "Sarah and Jason, could you please review the schedules for doing the business plan. I see all the options, but I wonder, if the Farmer's Market and Urban Garden don't work out for some reason, will we be back at the drawing board with another option? This process could go on for a long time before we find a social enterprise that works. In the meantime, we're living hand to mouth."

Jason stood up. "Great point! I'll take this one. You're correct. If we go through the exercise and decide, in the end, that we should not proceed, we will have spent considerable time and effort for naught. That's why we did the initial research and looked at different examples of success. While there is no guarantee, we think our matrix has helped us identify the best candidate for a social enterprise for our organization."

Michael added, "In addition to board members, here is a list of the people and other organizations or business we've already talked with to vet the idea."

- City of Phoenix – Neighborhood Services Department, George Lopez
- Farmer's Market Association – Phoenix, Sue Shore
- State Legislature Representative – Shirley Jenkins
- Independent Grocer – Louis LaGrange
- University of Arizona Extension – Master Gardener Program Manager – Henry Lee

"We've learned a great deal from these initial conversations, which we have documented and will use in our business planning."

"And the schedule will take us a year?"

"If our first idea works out, including obtaining financing, opening day would be a year from now. We believe we'll know if we should proceed with the Farmer's Market/Urban Garden after about sixty to ninety days when our market analysis is completed. If not, then within sixty to ninety days, we would re-evaluate our next move."

It was Sarah's turn to continue. "As I mentioned earlier, after many formats and iterations of business plans, I now use the following sections to write and organize a business plan."

"First, a section on the Market Opportunity. This section is external to NextPlace4Good and focuses on a broad view of the market. I then use a series of questions to narrow the field of play to an initial target. Every part of our plan uses the targeted segment and our understanding of it as a rationale for the initiative and its boundaries. As Jason mentioned, if we wouldn't see a viable market opportunity after the first sixty days, we would re-evaluate our approach."

"Once we define the Market Opportunity and our targeted segment within it, we develop a section that covers Our Initiative. After writing this section, we will have a very clear view of the business we are about to launch. We will have defined our value proposition, our offerings and a 360-degree view of how we will accomplish that. We will have a precise definition of our business model—that is how we will create, deliver and capture value. In the process, any gaps we might have in skills, experience, equipment, technology, etc. will be identified, along with ideas explaining how to close these gaps."

"The third section, Financials, models the initiative financially. We will look at all start-up expenses and then predict the growth of the business over time. In addition to the income statement, we will model cash flows.

This will give us an understanding of investments we might require from a social venture investor."

"That is what you will see when we're done. A market analysis our initiative to meet the market needs, and the financials that go along with the initiative. When we finish, we will summarize the plan in one page, which will be the first page, called the Executive Summary. Now I'll stop again for questions and comments."

Curt took the lead from there. "I think the team has given us their best shot at what will work to provide us a predictable revenue stream. I'd like someone to make a motion and a second."

The board approved the team to proceed and also installed the ad hoc committee. Jason, Sarah and Michael had worked long hours to get to this point. They agreed to come back at the challenge in a few days.

Jason spent a few minutes reviewing the notes he had taken and highlighted a few questions to ask Sarah.

Meeting notes

Business plan – get everyone on same page…communications + reduce risks (ask Sarah about)

Market Opportunity – how to define – ask Sarah?? Then 'our initiative' – know what it is…then financials. Get working on the Market opportunity… 60-day evaluation – do we have a viable opportunity?

ACTION: Schedule ad hoc committee meetings. Every 60 days – get meetings on calendar NOW.

Can we implement in less than one year to launch – find a way?

Two Steps Forward – One Step Back

The team met several days after the board meeting. Jason had made a list of near term commitments and, wherever possible, delegated responsibility to his staff so he could spend the maximum amount of time on the Farmer's Market/Urban Garden. Sarah and Michael praised his positive energy and smart prioritization.

It was Sarah's turn to define the next step of the process for them. She reiterated that they would be doing the Market Opportunity first, as she had discussed with them earlier and at the board meeting. At this meeting, she bluntly told them getting this part of the exercise right was absolutely critical to success. Typically, the analysis is a combination of quantitative and qualitative information. She wasn't sure how much real quantitative information would be available to them. They might be relying heavily on qualitative inputs from both knowledgeable people and focus group sessions.

Sarah explained, "We want to start with a broad look at the opportunity. How large is the overall market? How fast is it growing? These are indicators of overall health of the market."

"While we are probing the overall size and growth, we want to understand different ways the market might be segmented. What different characteristics might define it? Would it be the ability of the consumer to pay? Does the geography play a role? Where is the most need? We might want to subdivide the market by more than one characteristic. For example, where is the money spent and who spends it? What might we learn from each?"

Sarah concluded, "Let's set up a task and schedule to get to this point before we proceed further, okay?"

"Wow, now that we're actually doing this, where do we get this information?" Jason asked.

Sarah said, "That's part of the challenge, Jason. We will never have complete information, but we need to identify the best sources. I'm going to leave you with this as a challenge and see what you come up with. Don't worry. I'm not going to leave you in the lurch. You can call me when you have an idea, but it's important for you to really own the market analysis and understand it in great detail, so I want you to struggle a bit. To the degree you can do the market research, it also keeps my cost down. Does that make sense?"

While he didn't really think it made sense, Sarah didn't seem to give him another option. She also said she could be available if he needed to talk something through. So since Polly had been a business major and had taken Marketing courses, he decided to talk it over with her over the dinner table first.

"Where do I start?" Jason asked, after he had given Polly the gist of his assignment. "I've never done anything like this before, and I'm not sure what the research should look like when I'm done."

"Interesting situation sweetheart," Polly offered. "It's not like you will find market studies like in the cola market or automotive sales where market size and market shares are measured to the tenth of a percent. Most of my marketing courses covered the 4 P's of marketing. And, of course, we used examples like Coca-Cola or Crest toothpaste."

"And the 4 P's mean what exactly?"

"Product, Place, Price and Promotion, Jason. The courses drum that into your head until you remember it for life."

"I wish I had taken a few business courses now that I really need them."

"Well, you're a lucky ducky Jason. I have two more weeks of maternity leave, and I'm anxious to engage my brain, which has become mush. So I'll help you figure out how to develop a market size and segmentation for Farmer's Markets—and you'll owe me big time!"

"That's a deal! You're a lifesaver, and I already owe you big time, honey. But this is a debt I'm happy to pay." Jason breathed a sigh of relief.

The conversation ended when Isabella woke up from her nap, hungry for her next feeding.

At breakfast the next day, Polly showed Jason her notes. "I had a few ideas after last night's conversation, so I wrote them down. There is an approach we should take that I'm going to call 'tops down and bottoms up.' The tops down method is where we might find an article, or an association, or some market studies that would help us quantify the size and nature of Farmer's Markets. The bottoms up method, on the other hand, would require us to do a little scouting about where the Farmer's Markets are located around town. We'd need to talk to some of the vendors and get a sense of the business. Together we'd learn and be able to assemble a view of the market. This bottoms up method wouldn't be as precise, but it's probably as accurate as we need."

"I guess you did need something meaningful to think about since you've been home changing diapers for a month," Jason said, stating the obvious. "The tops down and bottoms up approach makes sense. It could even be fun for us as part of the bottoms up method to take Isabella out with us on Saturday morning and ride around town. Thanks sweetheart! I have to get to the office now. See you tonight."

During that morning, Michael checked in. He had taken the lead role in organizing the ad hoc committee and had drafted a short description of the committee's role and responsibility. He had also closed the loop with Howard as ad hoc committee Chairperson, and Curt as the board Chair. Jason asked Michael what he thought of the tops down and bottoms up approaches. Michael thought these two different approaches made sense, suggesting Jason might also check in with Sarah and ask her advice.

Sarah returned Jason's call early that afternoon. "I got your message. I was at a meeting all morning, but have time to chat now."

Jason said, "We, I mean I, have an idea I'd like to run by you and get your opinion." He then explained Polly's tops down and bottoms up approach.

Sarah replied, "Jason, absolutely, you're on track. We really don't know what this market is, so the first step is to really understand it. I feel strongly about identifying a particular segment of the market that will be our target. Do you think you can get there?"

"I think so, Sarah. I understand target marketing for real. I'm already getting bombarded with advertisements for baby paraphernalia, and Amazon is suggesting books I might be interested in. Businesses have targeted me as a new father for sure! I didn't receive these solicitations before, so they definitely segment new parents as a target."

"Well, I hope some of the solicitations are for things you want and need—not just annoying intrusions in your day. The tops down and bottoms up approach we just discussed will help us move up the learning curve. So good thought process, and keep in touch as you do your research. I can also suggest that you look at some of the government data that might be available from the U.S. Government. As taxpayers—individual taxpayers at least—the information is available to us and there's lots of it. The big trick is finding it. I'll call you frequently and see how you and Polly are progressing."

Michael and Jason had developed a strong friendship during the few months they had worked together. They respected each other's opinions and were both committed to the cause. Michael shared Jason's enthusiasm for the Farmer's Market idea and thought the Urban Garden was probably also a good thing even though perhaps not a high revenue producer. So one day, when Michael called unexpectedly, Jason could hear in his voice that something was terribly wrong.

"What is it, Michael?" Jason was instantly concerned. It sounded like Michael was barely holding it together.

"They found a lump when Jackie had her mammogram. And her doctor has scheduled a biopsy for later this week. There's no other information, but I'm a wreck. I think Jackie is holding it together for the kids and me. I have to bow out for a while Jason. I'd be no good to you in the state I'm in. Sorry to have to do this in the middle of the process."

"Wow, Michael, I don't know what to say. Of course, I hope everything is okay. But I understand, and I'll just keep working with Sarah. Please keep in touch. I hope you're back in the saddle soon."

"Thanks, Jason. I will keep in touch. If I could concentrate on anything, I'd come in and help. But right now, I'm a basket case and no help to anyone."

"If I don't hear from you, is it all right to call you?" Jason asked.

"Yes, call my cell. If I can't talk, it will be off. Just leave a message, and I'll call you back."

"Okay, good luck. I'll be thinking positive thoughts and sending positive energy in your direction, for both you and Jackie."

"Thanks, Buddy. Bye."

Jason leaned back in his chair and closed his eyes. Here he was with a new baby and the whole world going right. He wondered if he would have to face health challenges for himself or Polly, and whether he would also be a basket case. He decided yes, he, too, would be a basket case. After a while, Jason called the house. When Polly answered, Jason said, "I love you, Polly."

"Why, I love you too, Jason. But you don't usually call me from the office to say so. What's going on, honey?" Polly asked with surprise.

He relayed the phone call and how upset Michael was. Now Jason was upset, too. Polly suggested he call it a wrap at the office and come home. That evening, Jason sat quietly on the couch next to Polly, making sure he was close enough to feel her next to him. He wasn't really thinking much—just feeling bad about what Michael was going through.

SECTION 3:
Business Plan: The Market Opportunity

Speak With Data

The next morning Jason still wasn't in a great mood, but at least his head was a bit clearer. The reality that Michael—a key member of the core, three-member team was absent, cast gloom over his day. When Michael became involved with NextPlace4Good, Jason had been able to overcome the feeling of being overwhelmed. Now the feeling came back—and they had made commitments to the board to accomplish their scheduled milestones. Jason could barely think straight.

In a concerned but anxious voice, Jason called Sarah, explaining the situation to her. Sarah, also concerned about Michael, was able to calm and reassure Jason they would make their scheduled commitments. The two set up a meeting to go over the schedule and tasks to figure out what pieces needed attention while Michael was gone. Sarah also mentioned she was attending the Social Enterprise Alliance Conference out of town for a week, and had scheduled several other meetings while she visited Chicago.

Jason spent a nervous two days at the office worried that the organization could be imploding on his watch. First Michael had backed away and now Sarah would be unavailable during a critical time. At least Polly was making great progress identifying names and organizations of people to interview as part of the market sizing and segmentation.

After forty-eight hours that seemed like an eternity, it was time for Jason's meeting with Sarah.

Jason told Sarah that Polly was helping him with the market sizing. She had some great ideas, and he showed Sarah the list of contacts they were using:

1. Deborah – community leader in South Phoenix low-income food desert
2. Raoul – community leader in Phoenix in a low-income food desert
3. Liz at a local charitable trust that invests in healthier communities
4. Patti at a local foundation that supports capacity building and perhaps a social capital investor
5. Farmer's Markets in Phoenix and Scottsdale – pricing of stalls, other market economics of interest
6. Federal, state or local research – Michael at the U.S. Small Business Development Corporation (SBDC)
7. Academic research and press articles

The market data covered a variety of topics:
- Farmer's Market locations in the valley – competition
- Prices of produce compared to supermarkets
- Stall rental prices
- Food desert areas in the Valley
- Buying behavior of residents in Valley food deserts
- Residents needs and how to market to residents

Sarah explained that the market size would include opportunities for people to attain fresh fruits and vegetables. She pointed out that Farmer's Markets would serve a subset of those people and is a "slice" of the market. Additionally, the market size can be segmented by type of consumer:

families, older adults, low income, etc. This subset can be quantified with census data for the area.

Sarah took the data that Jason and Polly had researched and drafted a Market Opportunity section of the business plan. She shared the draft with Jason and Polly, reviewing each conclusion to be sure it was in sync with the data. Sarah encouraged them to edit the text or challenge the conclusions and not take the draft as final. After a few edits, the second draft looked pretty good.

DRAFT –   REV 2.0

The Market Opportunity (Full Market Opportunity Section included in Part 2)

The market opportunity to produce and sell affordable fresh produce will first be described in general to define its overall characteristics. Then specific market segments will be identified and, finally, a targeted segment will be identified for this business plan. The goal is to identify a need that NextPlace4Good can satisfy through an urban garden and Farmer's Market in a neighborhood that currently has limited access to affordable, fresh produce, otherwise called a food desert.

Overall Market Size and Growth Rates – This section covers size, growth and additional characteristics for low income neighborhoods with limited supermarket access, for food at home purchases and for Farmer's Markets as the retail outlet under consideration. These three dimensions are described for the U.S. as a whole and for the local Maricopa County (greater Phoenix AZ metropolitan area).

Food Deserts - Maricopa County AZ – The 2006 U.S.D.A. Food Atlas identified 55 census tracts as food deserts where 148,588 low-income residents (~5% of the population) live more than one mile from a supermarket and where 11,699 of those residents do not

---

have access to a car. Children ages 0-17 in poverty were 21.6% of the county population in 2010.

Food Security – Maricopa County AZ - The combination of *Food Insecure Households* averaged 15.3% between 2008-2010 and *Very Low Secure Households* averaged 5.9%, which totaled 21.2% of total households in the county. SNAP (Supplemental Nutrition Assistance Program) participation of the total population grew by a third between 2009–2011 to 16.47% and WIC (Women, Infants and Children Food and Nutrition Service) participation in the same period decreased a bit from 3.17% to 3.08%. Low-income preschool obesity between 2008-2010 was 14.9%.

Food at Home Market - Maricopa County AZ – the 2010 population was 3.817 million and continuing to grow but at a slower rate (1.65% in 2011) than the previous decade. Approximately 5% of the population in the county resides in a low income area more than a mile from a supermarket in a food desert. Using the federal guide for the average at-home food expenditure, each food desert census tract of approximately 4,000 residents would approximate $8,400,000 of annual spending for food at home.

Farmer's Markets - U.S. – Farmer's Markets have grown rapidly as the fascination with all things local and all things fresh has become popular. The farmer sets up a stand at a regularly scheduled market and sells direct to shoppers. Depending on the market, the farmer pays a small flat fee or a commission on sales. Farmers don't have to give payment terms or wholesale prices as they would to a store or restaurant, so more money stays in the farmer's pocket. Depending on the market, you may find yourself chatting with the farmer. The USDA's voluntary reporting of Farmer's Markets shows high growth.

Farmer's Markets - Maricopa County AZ – In 2011 there are 30 Farmer's Markets in Maricopa County, *none in low income communities* labeled as food deserts. Several local small farms are identified on a Local Harvest locator map within Maricopa County.

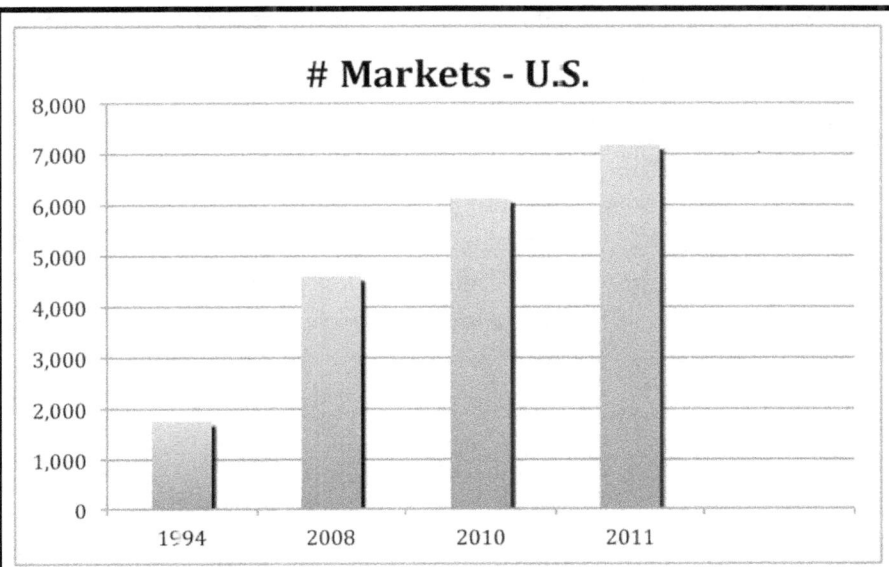

Markets - U.S.

Locally Grown Food – Maricopa County AZ - USDA records for 2007 identify 32 vegetable farms that harvested 17,472 acres, 180 orchards with 4,080 orchard acres, 129 farms that had farm direct sales and 31 farms that grew vegetables for fresh markets.

Market Segmentation – defining geographic areas with limited supermarket access and no existing farmer's market is the most relevant characteristic for our market. Additionally, the lack of access to a car and eligibility for government support programs plays an important role in segmentation.

Typical economics of the market segment – this section identifies the relevant dimensions that might influence buying at a Farmer's Market and a further clarification of the consumer need.

Competition – Currently residents who purchase fresh produce using SNAP EBT (electronic benefits transfer) cards travel 4.9 miles to a store. A Farmer's Market would provide a more locally accessible alternative for fresh produce. The competitive analysis is focused within the low income census tracts in our market segmentation analysis.

Our targeted market within the overall market opportunity – Our target is selected with three tiers, giving us a primary, secondary and tertiary source of customers. Tier 1 census tracts are our primary geographic target. The selection criteria includes only tracts in low supermarket access areas and is refined to select several adjacent census tracts that will provide a sufficient customer base for both EBT and retail purchases. A significant low income base, significant families with children base and a high percentage (>20%) without a car factored into the selection.

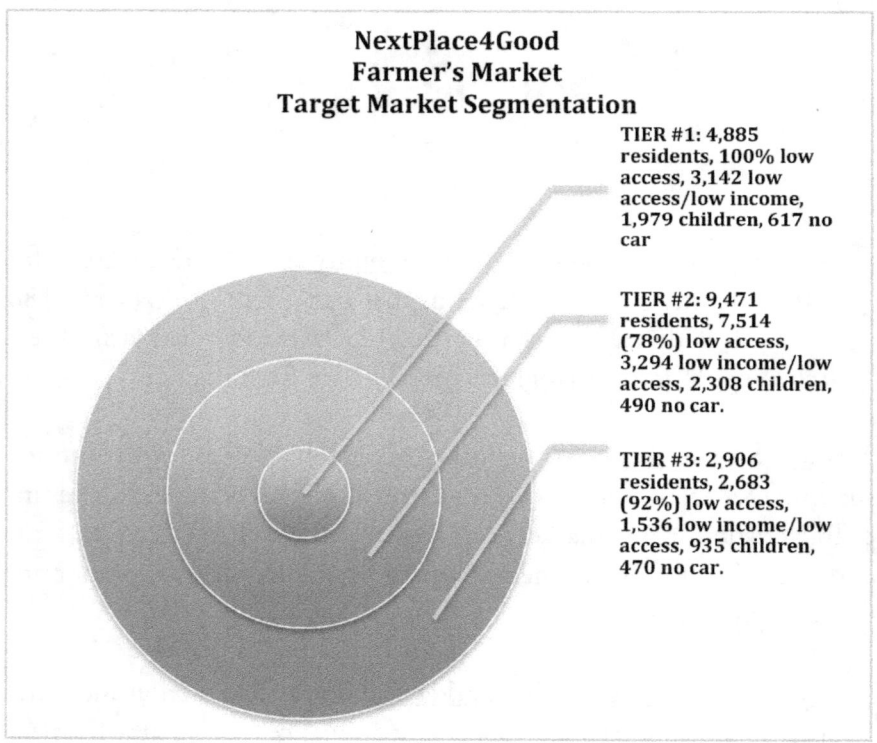

NextPlace4Good
Farmer's Market
Target Market Segmentation

TIER #1: 4,885 residents, 100% low access, 3,142 low access/low income, 1,979 children, 617 no car

TIER #2: 9,471 residents, 7,514 (78%) low access, 3,294 low income/low access, 2,308 children, 490 no car.

TIER #3: 2,906 residents, 2,683 (92%) low access, 1,536 low income/low access, 935 children, 470 no car.

The three tiers combined residential population of over 17,000 can easily sustain a Farmer's Market with the required weekly traffic and spending. The food-at-home expenditure approximates $35 million with a potential 6% or $2 million for Farmer's Markets and wholesale sales. To capitalize on this market opportunity requires serving the EBT and retail population with the availability, quality and price combination that is lacking in the neighborhood today.

In summary we have identified a market opportunity for fresh, affordable produce and believe we can build a successful business initiative around our target market segment.

Jason wished that Michael had been available to participate. Jackie had undergone the biopsy. The doctors had been quite optimistic, and when Jason spoke with Michael, he was worried, but better.

"They believe it's benign," he told Jason. "We've been nervous wrecks, especially me. I know someone who retired and within six months was diagnosed with cancer and three months later was gone. It's my worst nightmare to have worked so hard my whole life and not have the chance to enjoy this stage of life with Jackie."

"The results won't be back from the lab until next week," said Michael. "So we're going to drive up to Sedona and spend the rest of the week trying to relax. You can call me if you need anything. I'll let you know next week when to expect me back in the project."

"I can't even imagine what's it has been like for you, Michael," said Jason. "I'm happy to hear the doctors think it's benign. I hope you get confirmation of that quickly. Don't worry about us while you're in Sedona. Put your feet in the creek and have some nice dinners. Take lots of pictures of the red rocks and then come back energized. We'll be fine. Sarah and I will keep going. Polly has been helping out on the Market Analysis. We'll pretty much be on schedule. But I am looking forward to you being back soon. I'll admit that I was feeling a lot more secure when we were working together. So hurry back. You're needed here!"

"Thanks, Jason," Michael was getting choked up. "I'm a bit emotional about everything now, but we make a great team. It's good to hear you feel the same. I want to make our venture a success. I know we can, and I'll be back hopefully very soon!"

"I know, Michael. It will be soon, and we *will* succeed in this."

"Okay, partner," said Michael, getting a grip on his emotions. "Hope you get a lot done. So long for now."

"Yep, see you soon!"

Board Committee Still on Board

The next milestone was to review the Market Opportunity analysis with the Board's ad hoc committee. Sarah had insisted they publish the draft and a meeting agenda a week in advance of the meeting. "The board members are very busy people, Jason. We need to demonstrate the professionalism they expect of us—and we expect of them—by giving them the chance to review our work. We can then expect them to demonstrate a command of the topic, providing additional insights based on their professional experiences, which will benefit NextPlace4Good and this particular social enterprise venture."

Jason had been gun shy to send the document out before it had been thoroughly edited by him, Sarah *and* Michael, but Sarah had pushed to publish it anyway, insisting, "Getting it to them on time is more important than having it perfect. We sent it as a draft so it's okay if they catch a few typos. They'll understand that we're doing the business plan and running the day-to-day operations at the same time."

The meeting agenda included the objective of the session: to review the market research and analysis and to collect input from the committee members. Jason had briefed Howard in advance. The ad hoc committee also included Chuck child psychologist; Kathy, CPA; Julia, community leader; and Darren, high-tech marketing manager.

The meeting got off to a rocky start because committee members wanted to jump ahead to discuss the venture (revenues, hiring and aspects of the business plan), rather than provide feedback to the planning team. Jason and Sarah reminded them this first session was all about the external environment. Sarah kept a positive tone with the group because it was clear they saw the opportunity, but it was also important that the planning team (Jason, Michael and Sarah) receive sage advice from the board on the market opportunity. After the first hour and a few reminders, the committee settled into its role.

"If we meet the pricing requirements of the low income neighborhood, what makes us believe we can make money?" Kathy asked.

"Excellent question, Kathy," Jason responded. "While we don't know for sure, we have played with some booth rental numbers that suggest we can make money. The vendors can certainly make money and still price their products below the small neighborhood stores. These small stores carry mostly canned goods and only a few fresh items. Our prices would be roughly comparable to supermarket prices, which are well below typical suburban Farmer's Market prices. We also believe over time we can add prepared food, and perhaps crafts, that can support diversity and volume."

"What do you mean prepared food?" asked Chuck.

"It could, for example," said Jason, "include honey, fruit preserves, cheeses or sauces." Jason was describing some of the items he and Polly had seen in their Saturday market rounds.

Howard added, "I would hope we wouldn't end up being another Swap Meet where all kinds of useless trinkets get sold. We need to keep to the primary target of healthy foods available in so-called food deserts."

"You are so right, Howard," Kathy concurred. "Why not set a percentage, say, perhaps 80% of the booths sell fresh, affordable produce?"

Chuck and Darren nodded energetic approvals.

"So noted," Jason said. "That's exactly the type of guidance we're looking to get from the committee."

Howard now moved on to the double bottom line. "Let's talk a bit about the employees. Tell us about the work our clients will be doing, Jason."

"There will be a period of start-up, construction and training," began Jason. Then he went through the process of using the clients as employees, doing resume and interview training, then screening interviews and then hiring. Jason cautioned they had not yet focused on the details, but the business plan would identify the jobs available and include salary expense as part of the financial model.

The meeting was two hours long and covered a lot of ground. The more the committee members discussed items of interest, the more the positive energy toward the initiative grew. Their meeting ended on a high note when Howard announced, "This will be such a great win-win if, I mean *when,* we launch. Thank you Jason and Sarah for your work so far. On behalf of the committee, we want to encourage you to contact us during your next phase with any questions or concerns. We look forward to the next session."

"And one more thing: thank you for publishing the document for this meeting to us in advance. I know if I receive information like that just before the meeting, I may be too scheduled or out of town and unable to read it in advance. Having it in advance, I could plan time during the week to digest what you send, make my notes, consider questions, etc. The document was very professional by the way. Thank you for that."

"And our thanks to you for your thoughtful questions and comments," said Sarah, as she closed the meeting. "We will meet again in two months. At that time, you'll see a draft of the entire business plan. The business plan will serve as our explanation and guide for our proposed enterprise. It will also serve as a document to attract impact investors for our start-up funding requirements. These investors may be foundations or individuals. This means," Sarah concluded, "that our team has seven weeks to finish the plan so you receive it a week in advance!"

When they were alone, Jason gasped, "How *ever* are we going to finish this in seven weeks?"

"Not easily," Sarah laughed. "And you will need to be on this almost full time. But we'll do it. You'll see. I know you have a lot of the details in your head already. We just have to discuss them and document them. We'll be fine."

"If you say so. I'm counting on you to be right on this Sarah."

"I say so! Now let's go and have an evening off. Tomorrow will be a busy day."

SECTION 4:
Business Plan: Our Initiative to Meet the Market Opportunity

Getting Specific – Our Unique Value Proposition

Early the next day Sarah met Jason at the NextPlace4Good offices. They cloistered themselves in the conference room. Sarah opened her computer to review her notes and update their business plan action item log sheet. She explained the next step—the development of the Our Initiative section. This section captures in words how NextPlace4Good will meet the fresh produce needs identified in their market opportunity analysis. She was about to discuss the value proposition when the conference door opened and Michael stepped inside, a wide smile from ear to ear.

Their optimism proved true. After a hellish two weeks, Michael and his wife, Jackie, had received the best possible phone call from their doctor. Relieved beyond words, the couple had gone out for a celebratory dinner. Now Michael was back, ready to dig in to the project. The three of them high-fived and hugged, letting out the tension and relief. Jason and Sarah decided they should treat Michael to breakfast, using eating out as an opportunity to catch him up on progress and plans.

Michael listened carefully, asking them to repeat and explain some of the research, especially on the economic business model. He was the only board member so far that did not jump right in to asking questions about the venture. Instead, he asked questions about the market analysis, absorbing every data point in their charts and noting where he still had open questions.

"It's always been my habit to understand who my customers might be, what their buying behavior is or could be, and how I could meet a need they have. Only after I feel that I understand the customer's buying habits well enough do I plan the business to fulfill a market need. The challenge is to know when enough research is enough because you never get one hundred percent knowledge. At some point, I trust my experience and move forward."

Sarah and Jason were now all ears, having great respect for Michael's experience and track record of success in business.

"So I know we're on a tight time line," Michael said, "and I'm not suggesting we delay, but I do have a suggestion. We all have an intuitive sense that there is a market failure to sell fresh food in these low income areas and that we can train our clients to capably work in a business that grows and sells quality, affordable produce. We believe it's a win for our organization, our clients and the community."

Sarah and Jason agreed.

"I can envision ways we can learn more while we build the business," said Michael. "We can stage our growth so that we are able to take less risk and get the business set on the right track. What if we focus on our production first and exhibiting at other local Farmer's Markets? We could enroll a number of our youth at the Master Gardener program at the extension of the University of Arizona. We could also recruit experts in the area to volunteer or be paid a small stipend to launch our food production. There's a lot to learn in just this part of the business, but it does offer us revenue opportunities even early on."

Jason and Sarah listened intently as Michael continued with his ideas. "We could rent a booth at another market first, before we open our own Farmer's Market, and gain experience over the first six or nine months. We would have the experience of selling in the market and the time to further understand our local customer. Then we will be ready to implement our own market, recruiting other local farmers as vendors. We could even think about an intermediate step of having just a farm stand close to our garden before the complete Farmer's Market. What do you think of planning in stages and learning as we go?"

"I get what you're thinking, Michael." Jason was now leaning over the breakfast table. "We could get to the same place two or three years down the road, but take it in stages, learn the pieces of the business and get them in place as we go. Wow, I think that's a great idea! What do you think, Sarah?"

"Makes perfect sense and we can build our initiative that way—around a staged business development."

After the long breakfast, Sarah became the taskmaster. "We're on a short time line to get a draft of the initiative completed. It will be best to go back to the conference room to begin our discussions now."

With full stomachs but much lighter hearts, all three returned to the office and Sarah relaunched the discussion about a value proposition.

"The business model describes how we create, deliver and capture value. The value proposition is in the center of the business model," she began. It defines the value you bring, that your customers are willing to *pay* for, and that is distinctively yours, differentiated from what others might do in a similar enterprise."

"So if we say we are employing homeless youth, is that distinctive?" Jason asked.

"It might be," Sarah responded. "And many might pay because the money goes to a good cause. Although as I remember discussions I've had with social entrepreneurs, that hasn't been enough. But if we can separate ourselves from a charitable donation mindset and adopt a business mindset, there is a value proposition that is related to our enterprise, I believe. Answering some questions might help."

She wrote on the whiteboard – Value Proposition:
1. What is it?
2. How will the value proposition impact the buyer?
3. Why we are uniquely qualified to deliver this value proposition?
4. What is the sustainable competitive advantage?

"Not sure here. Uh . . . we produce and sell fresh produce at affordable prices in food deserts of Phoenix, Arizona?"

"Yes, that's the gist. We might want to say 'produce, sell and host a market place for fresh produce.' That might include the products of others. What do you think is our sustainable competitive advantage?"

"I have no clue. What does that mean?"

"It asks why someone else can't open a similar business across the street and take our business from us?"

"One reason is we are a nonprofit. Our returns can be lower and don't need to satisfy shareholders."

"Great point! Anything else come to mind?"

"Does our commitment to the community and our clients count in this?"

"Excellent thought. That does give the definition additional clarity. Perhaps that's enough on the value proposition. We're in draft mode, so we can come back if we decide anything else."

Michael broke his silence while Jason was thinking through the value proposition. "Let's capture what we've said so far: *NextPlace4Good, through its workforce development programs, grows, sells and hosts a market place for affordable fresh produce that is accessible in low income communities.* Is that what we're saying?"

"Yes, excellent again. It captures the nonprofit part and employing those with barriers to employment. Next we want to describe our *offerings* to meet the needs of the segment we identified in our market analysis."

"Offerings, okay. How about this:
1. We grow greens, tomatoes, carrots, melons and fresh vegetables for sale.
2. We participate in a Farmer's Market on Saturday and Wednesday.
3. Maybe longer term, we produce and sell other food products like preserves, honey or salsas—also flowers.
4. We host a farm stand and/or a Farmer's Market."

"Is that what you mean?"

"Pretty close. It feels like the Farmer's Market produces the largest, predictable revenue stream. We should state it as our primary business, even though we get there in stages. Having our produce for sale will complement the revenues, but I wonder if we weren't going to do a Farmer's Market would we still do an Urban Garden?"

"Good question. I'm not sure. The revenue might be an issue but the employment of our clients would still count."

"Point well taken. Final question: how is our offering differentiated from others?"

"Why do we have to be differentiated? It's a Farmer's Market like many others."

"That's just it. What would make customers come to you instead of another Farmer's Market? What is special about yours? Think back to our market opportunity work. What did the people you interviewed say?"

"Ah, they wanted a special place, a community place. Thinking out loud, maybe we make it special, like a Mercado with ethnic food, music, games for kids—stuff like that. Our young employees might like that too. Perhaps the kids even help out in the garden and learn about growing food, as well as the importance of healthy eating."

"There you go. If you look back at our competition analysis, we said our strength would include education, fun and community, in addition to convenience. I think we have enough to keep going. Some great ideas are coming out of this discussion to factor in the Our Initiative section."

"Here's the task, Jason. I'm going to give you a list of questions. Think about these the way we've discussed the value proposition and offerings. Then the three of us will meet again and develop the 'answers' that will go in our business plan."

Jason took the question template home and drafted his own thoughts for each question. He needed input on a few from Sarah and Michael, but he actually felt like he could visualize the business. As he answered the questions, the approach to take became clear. With Michael's major insight—the need to develop the production and garden first, and use existing Farmer's Markets as the initial stage of a business—Jason made great progress. He could see the opportunity to train and employ his clients, enabling them and the organization to learn *and* earn revenue. As a second stage of the development, he could expand and launch his own Farmer's Market in an underserved area of the city.

Jason's Homework Questions and Answers

As a reminder and reinforcement for the questions, Jason wrote draft statements of the value proposition and offerings.

Value Proposition Draft:
NextPlace4Good, through its workforce development programs, grows, sells and hosts a marketplace for affordable fresh produce accessible in low income communities.

Offerings Draft:
We host a weekly Farmer's Market in a local food desert, offering fresh produce grown by our workforce (clients) and others in a fun, educational and community-minded environment.

We build this business in stages, with the first stage being workforce development of homeless youth to grow and harvest an urban community garden. The next stage will be produce sales at other existing Farmer's Markets. Ultimately, our enterprise will host our own Farmer's Market.

After our Farmer's Market is financially viable, we may extend our reach into prepared foods for sale.

"Business Model Definition: A business model describes the rationale of how an organization creates, delivers and captures value . . .

. . . This works in both for profit and tax exempt environments. The creation of value is the product or service that is designed and replicated in a standard or customized fashion. The delivery is the sale or application of the product or service. Value capture is more easily measured in a for profit environment by an income statement, balance sheet and cash flow statement where all activities are expressed in dollars. The value in a nonprofit should include a 'bottom line' profit margin, but also includes an outcome measure where the client and/or community are improved . . .

. . . The business model canvas co-developed in the book Business Model Generation identifies the elements necessary in a business model and how they relate to each other to actualize the definition."

Business Model Generation, 2010, Osterwalder & Pigneur

Business model design – What are our basic *assumptions* about pricing, expenses, and margins? (This is not the financial plan, which comes later.)

Answer: Our first priority will be to obtain an acre of vacant land with access to water, visibility from the street, access to public transportation and parking availability. The street visibility and parking will be attributes when we have a true market. The acre and water are necessary to launch our garden. When we identify locations, we will assist landowners, if it's privately owned land, to receive property tax abatements to let us use their land. We will attempt to share the cost of the water.

We will focus on growing fresh, affordable food. Our pricing in our first stage, selling in existing Farmer's Markets will be approximately 75-90% of the Farmer's Market prices to offset our more limited variety and quantities versus local farm vendors. We will need to hire an expert in farming that will train and supervise our clientele and help with production planning. Our existing staff will be able to identify potential candidates for Master Gardener training at the University of Arizona extension program. We will need to identify clean clothing, shower facilities and transportation for our clients for training, as well as employment.

Our initial marketing will be an attractive tabletop booth and signage for an existing Farmer's Market. Additionally, we will need signage for the garden to let residents and drivers know what's happening.

When we are ready to expand to our own Farm Stand or Farmer's Market, we will obtain a grant for start-up expenses and construction. We will attract neighborhood dollars that are currently going outside the neighborhood for food purchases, thereby saving the consumer transportation costs. We will partner with entertainers and offer other fun activities as incentives for neighbors to shop at our market. To recruit local farmers, we will provide transportation of their produce to our market, and we will even staff their booth as additional revenue opportunities. We will accept WIC and SNAP EBT cards and will need working capital to support the time lag in the cash cycle. Over time, in addition to straight sales, we will have prepared food—baked goods, sandwiches and drinks—that can have a higher price and margin. We will charge other vendors a booth fee of 10% of their expected sales, which will contribute more revenue.

We will partner with others that have a mission to promote healthy eating and active living, as well as offering fun opportunities that also build community.

We will develop a plan that can train, pay and supervise our youth while still achieving positive cash flow after a two year start-up period. The first two years will require subsidy and start-up funding, which we will have to obtain. We will have to engage a food safety resource and also obtain the proper insurances. We will achieve industry average margins in our third year.

Implementation – What are the assumptions about implementation, for example, staggered versus all-at-once or start-up with all products and services versus selected-for-target-market segment? Are there any other important assumptions to call out?

Answer: We will focus on our production first and then exhibiting at other local Farmer's Markets. We will enroll our youth who are selected at the Master Gardener program at the extension of the University of Arizona. We will recruit experts in the area to volunteer or be paid a small stipend to launch our food production, and we will rent our own booth at another market to gain experience over the first six to nine months. Then we will implement our own market in an underserved area of the valley that is on our garden land or adjacent to it. We anticipate that by the beginning of Year 2 we will at least have a Farm Stand on our property, if not a full Farmer's Market. By the end of Year 3 we expect to have a fully operational and cash flow positive Farmer's Market.

What is *outside the scope* of our business model design?

Answer: Hire and train existing clients to the degree possible. What we'd like to be outside the scope is hiring people who are *not* clients. Keep longer range vision in mind even though business development has to occur in stages. Processed foods and food aggregation are beyond the reach of our enterprise.

Implementation Scope -- This is descriptive rather than quantitative to call out key requirements and gaps that will be filled in our implementation plan.

Marketing - How will we go to market?

Answer: We will first identify specialty produce that we can sell at the Central Phoenix Farmer's Market. We want to produce to the market demand, including ethnic foods where appropriate, for example, okra, kale, peppers, bok choy, etc. Once we select the produce, we will decide how to display it on a tabletop and develop colorful, portable signage at different elevations so that it's attractively presented. We will also develop price tags and brochures about our urban garden for those interested. We will also provide brochures about NextPlace4Good. Initial marketing will be at the existing sites of Farmer's Markets. Depending on the quantity we produce, we will go to either one or two markets per week. Additionally, we will have permanent attractive signage with street visibility in front of our garden.

What are the key marketing activities?

Answer: We need to complete Market Research on what to grow that will sell at the Central Phoenix Farmer's Market. We will also need a logo and pictures for our tabletop at the market, as well as signage and presentation at the market.

What are the requirements to succeed?

Answer: Sell what we produce with limited spoilage, shrinkage and discounting. Create an awareness of our brand that is positive, inclusive and memorable.

Where are our key gaps?

Answer: Dedicated resources and a budget to accomplish signage, presentation, brochures and a logo and business name.

When he looked up to check the time, Jason was amazed that it was 1:00 a.m. He had become so absorbed in thinking through the aspects of the business each question required that he completely lost track of the time. He looked in on the baby and thought, "That's what it means to sleep like a baby," knowing that she would be waking up soon for a meal. He dragged himself into bed, realizing he'd never get enough sleep to be effective tomorrow, but satisfied with his progress on his homework.

Field Trip – Learning From Others

Their next work session was at Sarah's office to get away from the constant interruptions. Jason had emailed his answers to them in advance. He could tell they had read his homework. Each copy had notes written in the margins.

Sarah began. "Excellent thoughts. This is the level of detail we should have in the business plan. This is so-o-o important that I want to talk each section through as a team. But let's cover each section in order, share ideas, and spend most of our time today on Marketing, making sure we're clear on what's required as we grow the business."

"As you can see, most of my notes are in the Business Model section, getting more specific based on the business model from other successful ventures."

Michael added, "Same here. I wanted to suggest that we look for other affordable transportation options from farms to market. That will keep us focused on the core purpose of the enterprise. It will also be less complicated and costly for us since transportation requires a truck, insurance and trained drivers."

"Hmmm, I see your point."

Sarah continued, "I researched several mature urban Farmer's Markets and found them to be nicely profitable at 15% of sales or more. Most earn revenues from fees, but in certain cases, they sell their own produce to a minor degree. Spoilage is one of the major expenses and can get out of control, if not well managed. When produce is sold, it appears that a 50% markup is applied to the cost. So for every dollar of production cost, the sell price would be $1.50. Then all the other expenses would have to total 30 - 35% in order to breakeven."

They had good discussion on the business model design and staggered implementation that they all embraced. They made corrections, including outsourcing transportation, but showered Jason with positive recognition and reinforcement for his work.

When they started talking about Marketing, Sarah said what Jason covered seemed on target—the brand, the signage, and the brochure. In addition, she added that an understanding of their customers and developing the right communications just for their target customers was critical to their success.

Michael added, "I came across this article. It covers all kinds of ideas on selling at Farmer's Markets. Look at the pictures of displays, how they are arranged in a three-dimensional way and how appetizing it is! I made copies for each of us." The article was a compilation of twenty pages of articles on different topics, all-important for the team.

They discussed each of the "Top 10 Rules of Market Displays", including good signage, cleanliness and interacting with customers.

After a productive work session, Sarah summarized all they achieved so far: they had a solid handle on the market and a good start on the initiative, but they still needed to work through more elements of what's involved at the business plan level before they tackled the financials.

"For the next portion of defining the Our Initiative," she suggested, "I would like you to meet with a client who finished his business plan and launched a social enterprise a little over two years ago—recently enough to remember the process, but with the experience about what worked and what he would do differently. He's agreed to cover our next topics of management, human resources, technology, facilities, organization capability and any other infrastructure questions we have. He can also be a sounding board for the amount of start-up capital and working capital we might need until we become cash flow positive."

The NextPlace4Good business plan team met with John Miller, CEO of Second Chance, a Tucson AZ nonprofit that provided residential treatment for addiction. They had been highly dependent on government funding to treat an uninsured low income population, but as their salaries, benefits and other costs went up, the government reimbursements did not. John met the team at the reception area of his treatment facility. "Thanks for driving the two hours to see our facility. I'm happy to spread the benefits of earned income enterprises in the tax exempt sector—and notice I didn't say nonprofit sector."

"Seeing is believing. As we walk around our facility, I'll show you the several businesses we've launched as money makers for us and, in many cases, job training and employment opportunities for our residents."

"I'm sure Sarah explained our situation several years ago. It was a classic case of 'no money, no mission' and we were in a negative spiral of cost cutting and service reductions just to survive. The first initiative Sarah helped us plan and launch was to qualify for insurance reimbursements. This enabled us to treat a new segment of the population at reimbursements that do cover our costs. With the extra breathing room, we were able to identify opportunities that are triple plays. They meet a market need; they provide employment for our clients in recovery; and after the start-up period, the enterprises contribute to the Second Chance revenue and profit."

Continuing the tour, they saw the proof. "Here is our men's wing. If you look through the classroom window, you see training for our janitorial services business. Likewise, now we're in the women's wing, and you see a classroom for nail techs in salons. We have our own salon in the neighborhood. We manage it, and our residents work there—at least until they're ready to move to our bridge housing or back to their families. So that's what we do for now. This enterprise is working so well that we are constantly looking at new business opportunities."

They arrived at the conference room where John had left copies of the business plans that he and Sarah had developed for each venture. "I brought these as reference, in case I needed to show you anything to answer your questions. We're proud of them, and I also like to show them off," he chuckled.

"I'm proud, too, and I'm VERY proud of you and the team at Second Chance," Sarah responded. "It was a good idea to have the plans as references and be able to show Jason and Michael a few examples. Let's briefly review our NextPlace4Good market research and the value proposition, offerings and approach." Then Sarah explained they would like his advice on the human resource, technology, facilities and any other upfront requirements.

"So I see you're at the point in your planning to really think through how your operation will look when it's successful. And I would say from experience to first think about your management and leadership needs, followed closely by other skilled resources. For example, do you have a profile of the person to lead the enterprise? What would be the skills, experience and leadership traits that would be ideal?"

"I was thinking about one of our clients as the leader," offered Jason.

"Perhaps you have someone, but if you go wrong with the leader, it's hard to be successful with the venture. You're better off selecting the right leader, even if that isn't a client of your organization. Get it?"

"Yes, I see what you're getting at. I hadn't really thought about adding another professional to the staff."

"Well, I would encourage you to do so. Here, look at our business plan for the insurance business. Here's the profile we outlined and ended up hiring someone who had worked with insurers in the substance abuse treatment arena for twenty years. Her knowledge saved us time, money and mistakes. For you, that would be someone . . ." he thought for a moment, "someone who understood community gardens and how to hire, train and grow produce for sale."

"Got it. Good idea."

"Next, you'll need to think about the attributes of good workers and the job requirements. Since you described how you will need to provide unusual benefits for homeless youth, like shower facilities and work uniforms, you need to consider all these items as part of your human resource planning. Would you consider conducting a focus group of your clients to identify what would make a gardening job attractive to them? See where I'm going with this? You really have to envision this as a business that's already running. You don't have to get into specifics yet. That comes with the project implementation plan. But you do need to identify key gaps, especially items that will cost money so you include it in your start-up costs."

They took a quick break. Michael approached John, congratulated him on the success of his social enterprises and thanked him for his counsel to the team. "No problem," John said. "I'm happy to spread the word on social enterprise. Wish more nonprofits would think about earned income. When we reconvene, I want to show you how we're leveraging technology in our ventures."

A young man in a white kitchen uniform brought in fresh coffee and a baked goods tray.

At the end of the break John asked, "Did you enjoy the blueberry scones?"

"Yes, John, they were excellent. Where did you buy them?"

"From our kitchen. George, who brought the food cart, also baked them this morning. It's part of his job training in our commercial kitchen. Of course that's where we cook for our residents, but it serves a second purpose as preparation for jobs in the food services industry. And there's a gleam in our mind's eye that we might have a catering enterprise someday—success breeds all these other new venture ideas. The whole thing is contagious. Beware!"

They all laughed and inwardly hoped to catch the contagion.

"Well, Sarah wanted me to talk about automation and our use of technology. Our insurance initiative forced us into using a system that complied with the major insurance companies. It was a major investment in both money and time to get it right. We had to borrow the money, so we were careful about how we spent it. That's a good lesson, even if you're going after grant dollars for start-up."

"So at first we really had no choice but to invest in technology upfront, if we wanted to be paid. But we learned. Then when we were planning our janitorial services, it didn't require technology. But we'd built our confidence and our experience, so we asked ourselves, what are automation requirements? What are information and reporting requirements? What are financial system requirements? We included technology tools and enablers in our early thinking."

"But did you understand what you needed before you started?" asked Michael. "And if so, how did you know?"

John continued, "Good question, and clearly our system today is more robust than Day One, and next year our system will be improved again. The terrific thing about technology that's available is that the software is so-o-o flexible, it can grow as you do. Even how you purchase it can be flexible. So what we did know was that we wanted excellent customer interfaces with our janitorial services. The building managers require specific information to process purchase orders and invoices. We made sure we got it right so we got paid promptly. Customers appreciate the accuracy as well. Then we were also able to develop our reporting for our board and ourselves. We developed a dashboard of key performance measurements to track our progress versus our goals and gave us early warning of problems."

"So, Sarah, does that cover what you wanted?"

"Perfect, John. We're in a somewhat different environment, but with its own needs. For example, we'll have batches of kale; bags of spring mix greens, individual melons, etc. as inventory. And we'll need to track inventory, as well as the cash, from our Farm Stand and Farmer's Market. So the learning process you experienced is what we'll be talking about when we think through our approach, right gentlemen?"

"Right!" they said in unison.

"Great, I'm glad our experience can be of some value to you. The final topic Sarah asked me to cover was facilities. Wow, we'll be way different there too. What can I say that might help? I guess I can offer advice—free advice, so take it for what you paid for it."

"My advice is to figure out what you'll need. Don't under budget, but, when you're actually spending the money, be very cautious and penny pinch. I say this because you want clean and functional but not extravagant. And you won't get everything right the first time. So rather than have to raise or borrow more money, save some of it for do-over's."

"Oh, one more thing, Jason. When you're working with Sarah on the financials, and she's asking you about start-up costs, make sure you include the working capital you'll need, as well as other equipment and facilities."

"Can you say more about that?"

"Sure. What I mean is that you'll have lots of expenses before you earn enough to cover those costs. For instance, as you start your garden, you'll need seed, water and workers. You'll always have to pay for those before you sell the produce you grow. So that cash outlay would be working capital."

"Thanks, John, for your advice and for this whole morning. I feel like I'm drinking from a fire hose, but I took copious notes. I really, really appreciate you taking the time to meet with us and share your experiences."

"I want you to be successful, and I know you will be. You have terrific support in Sarah and Michael. Your organization has a critical mission. Every kid you turn into a productive citizen is important to our community. Call me anytime to ask a question or just talk. And I'll be following your progress with great interest."

SECTION 5:
Business Plan: The Financial Model

Matching Dollars to Activities

In the two-hour ride back from Tucson to Phoenix, both fellows were effusive about the opportunity to talk with John as someone who was open to sharing his knowledge and experience with them.

"John is characteristic of the social enterprise movement, if I can call it that," said Sarah. "While he was doing his business plan, I introduced him to a fellow CEO in Chicago who was two years ahead of John in his implementation. He was able to get advice, avoid mistakes and build his confidence during the planning process. So in his mind, meeting with us was part of his obligation to the movement. And when we're successful, you will be asked to give your advice to others too! You'll be called individually, asked to participate in conference workshops, perhaps even give speeches."

"While we're on the topic of conferences and workshops, I want to encourage, maybe insist, that we all attend the Social Capital Market (SOCAP) conference in San Francisco. Jason should actually apply as a social entrepreneur for a SOCAP scholarship to the conference and deliver a three-slide presentation to an audience of social impact investors.

It will sharpen our focus, and we'll get expert advice and feedback. I can also make appointments with the impact investors who attend. They are potential investors in our enterprise, either now or in the future, and we can begin developing a relationship with them."

"Do you think we'll be ready by then?"

"If we sign up for the conference and set up appointments with investors, we certainly *will be* ready! It can act as a forcing function for us to finish the planning process."

Impact Investing:

"Impact investments are investments made into companies, organizations, and funds with the intention to generate measurable social and environmental impact alongside a financial return. Impact investments can be made in both emerging and developed markets, and target a range of returns from below market to market rate, depending upon the circumstances. Impact investors actively seek to place capital in businesses and funds that can harness the positive power of enterprise. Impact investing occurs across asset classes, for example private equity/venture capital, debt, and fixed income.

Impact investors are primarily distinguished by their intention to address social and environmental challenges through their deployment of capital. For example, criteria to evaluate social and/or environmental performance are an integrated component of the investment process."

Source: Wikipedia

"By the way, we have another forcing function sooner than that. When we get back to the office, we need to review our meeting schedule and make sure we're ready for the ad hoc board committee review that's four weeks from now. We've made great progress, but still need to complete the planning on our initiative and develop the financial model. We've promised to get them materials a full week in advance of the meeting, which gives us three weeks to finish the work toward the package we send them. The financials never work out the first or even second time. Don't be discouraged. It's not us. It's the process. Financial planning is always an iterative process between what we want to do and what we can afford. But in the end, you'll thank me."

"Sure hope so. We're counting on it."

"I promise. This is the time when it looks impossible to finish, much less finish on time. But we will, and the plans will all make sense. You will be proud to present your business plan. That's my promise. Have faith. I've been through this enough times to know we're on a great track."

"There's something about the financials I don't understand. Can one of you explain? How do we know what to put down? Do we just make up the numbers? It seems so arbitrary."

"I'll take this one, Sarah." Michael jumped into the conversation. "It'll keep me alert as I drive. People who do many financial models forget that not everyone has had that experience. So it's good that you asked, Jason. You'll also be able to understand why Sarah described it as an iterative process. Let's start with the urban garden. We'll find the right location, with the right street frontage, parking, water, etc. It'll be a vacant lot, and if it's privately owned land, we'll work with the landowner to lease the property. He'll benefit from reduced property tax, and we'll have our site. Even before we've found the exact site, we'll be able to estimate with reasonable accuracy—doesn't have to be perfect—the costs for the lease and any improvements we'd need to make.

Then we'll have to estimate how many of our youth we will hire, train and employ. We'll have costs associated with each of these activities. Then we'll have the start-up costs of our garden. We'll either have to rent or build a place for our youth to stay. We'll probably need to purchase work clothes, boots, tools, seed, the farm stand itself and we'll be able again to estimate those expenses.

Part of our iterations will be to try to think of all the expenses we will have and get a reasonable, realistic estimate of each one. This is all before we harvest a single crop. Then we know we'll have to raise that amount of money to get going. Or if we don't believe we can raise that amount of money, we'll need to go back through our start-up costs to see what we can defer or eliminate. For awhile after we harvest, we will certainly have expenses that are greater than the sales we might make."

"I think I get how we can list all our start-up costs and somehow be able to afford them, but how do we develop the revenues?" Jason asked.

"It will be awhile before the cash we take in from produce sales will be as much as we're spending—before we reach a breakeven point," said Michael. "Your question about making up numbers relates more to how we project our sales, and that's where more iteration takes place. Our initial business is to sell produce at another Farmer's Market. Let's say we have our food production plan. We're ready to harvest carrots, green onions, cantaloupes, etc. We estimate the quantity we have to sell, our prices, and how much we will sell at the Central Phoenix Farmer's Market, as well as the costs of going to the market. We might talk with other vendors to get their input and watch the traffic at the market: how much customers spend, and on what, before we participate. We look at how quickly we can ramp up production and how increased production can turn into increased sales."

Jason was following Michael's explanation intently.

"Financial modeling is more of an art form than a science, but there are a couple of insights we will gain. First, we'll need to identify actions we must take to realize our sales targets. For instance, these actions might be marketing, or they might be additional training or uniforms for our youth. The actions may lead to additional expenses, or we may choose to reduce our sales targets. Second, it will take a few times through to see in our mind's eye what business will look like in Year 2 and Year 3 that will be part of our financials. That's a long way off from now, and we'll have to think through how we grow, how fast, where the funding will come from, all that. In the end, after multiple versions, we will have a plan and a matching financial model that we've talked through. We understand what we have to do, and we'll have confidence that we can achieve it. How's that for Sarah-like confidence."

"Great Michael!" Sarah smiled. "Couldn't have said it better myself. Just to emphasize what Michael said: part of the process is to identify what we need to accomplish to achieve our financial targets, to convince ourselves those actions are realistic and will result in meeting the financial targets, and to keep tweaking the financials until that is true—until realistic actions match a realistic target. Did that help Jason?"

"Thanks. Generally, it did, but I'll need to have you walk me carefully through the financials. This is not my area. Since we're pulling into the parking lot, why don't we go in and make sure we have enough time scheduled together before the business plan has to go out to the ad hoc committee."

SECTION 6:
Business Plan: The Review

Board Committee **Not** on Board

A few short weeks later, the NextPlace4Good ad hoc board committee members assembled for this review. They had full attendance, a positive signal to Jason that he would have their support to positively influence the entire board.

"Michael and I have now covered our market analysis, and how we're going to meet a critical market need with our social enterprise," said Jason.

Almost immediately, Michael noticed Kathy's body language and angry look when everyone else appeared to be fully engaged in the discussion. "What was she thinking?" he wondered.

Jason continued. "Before I ask Sarah to comment on the financials, I will walk us through two important sections of our business plan; first, our organization capability and second, our risk assessment. To prepare ourselves for success, Sarah asked a number of penetrating questions about our skills and expertise: what we have and what we'll need. She pushed us to identify where we have gaps. Based on our discussions as a planning team, I want to highlight two new positions we need to fill immediately. First, we need to hire a part time Master Gardener who can work with our client employees to grow produce. This is someone with farming knowledge who can do the production planning and also has the leadership skills to train and supervise our client employees. If we're lucky that person would have marketing skills as well, but production and supervision are critical. Second, we also need a Business Manager whose first tasks will be to set up our systems and controls and team with the Master Gardener to hire the right client employees and get them trained."

Jason then focused board members' attention on the main reasons for the new hires: "These two individuals will be 100% focused on our social enterprise. Selecting the right two people will be critical. We envision the part-time Master Gardener becoming full time in six to nine months."

Jason reviewed the overall hiring plan, as well as new business systems and processes, such as cash management and internal controls. He mentioned what key performance indicators they would measure to track their expected progress.

Howard, attorney and Committee Chair, chimed in: "You know, we should also consult with one of my friends who works a lot with tax exempt legal and tax implications. We want to incorporate this with the right legal structure from the get-go. That should be one of our action steps as we begin."

Michael agreed. "Absolutely, Howard, and I'm glad you know who to contact. We needed to understand the market and get our planning done first, but we know the relationship with the NextPlace4Good 501(c)(3) also needs to be discussed. We don't want to do anything that might jeopardize our tax exempt status of the primary nonprofit."

Darren took a turn as well, saying, "While we're suggesting ideas and resources, in the past, my company has offered up some of us in the Marketing Department to be available for charitable projects. We could take advantage of that offer at NextPlace4Good. Some of my colleagues would love to get their hands on a start-up project like this. They could help with logos, branding, brochures, and all the marketing collateral that we'll need. We would actually define the scope of work and deliverables the same way as an in-house project. Management allows us to use work time. They view it as team building within the company, as well as helping the community."

Before Jason could acknowledge and accept Darren's idea, Kathy jumped in with her concerns: "I'm amazed that we're actually talking about spending so much money, not to mention hiring new people! We just went through a major cost-cutting period just to stay open. As a board member and a CPA, I take our fiduciary responsibility very seriously. I am totally against going forward with this social enterprise venture until we're in a better financial situation."

The other board members did not see this coming. Community leader Julia spoke first: "Kathy, I understand your concerns. Let's talk this through. I don't see Jason or Michael or Sarah suggesting irresponsible financial risks here. We all know what they've been working on. It's now time to get specific about what it takes to be successful, don't you think?"

Sarah felt her outsider consultant role could help to calm and facilitate the discussion. "Thanks Kathy and Julia for your comments. It's important for us as a planning team to hear your thoughts even critical ones, so that we can address those concerns. Perhaps Kathy could say a bit more about where she thinks we've run off the rails with what we've proposed. Kathy?"

"I think you ran off the rails months ago by even thinking we could launch a new business when we can hardly keep the doors open. We should be hunkering down until the economy improves and our donations grow again. I also don't think we should be funding you as a consultant at this time. I especially don't approve of hiring two new people, even though one is only part-time, when we've just made cutbacks in direct service personnel. Is that clear enough, Sarah?"

You could hear a pin drop in the conference room. All were taken aback. Sarah knew she had to think quickly and draw out the others. 'If I understand correctly, Kathy is suggesting that we should not be working on this business plan. We should be focused on the core organization instead. I'd like to hear everyone else's view. Who would like to start?"

Chuck, child psychologist, had been particularly quiet so far, but he raised his hand first: "While I agree the board needs to be fiscally responsible, I'm confident we have been up to this point. I also have confidence that we will continue to be responsible in the future. I'm not a businessperson and can't judge how good the planning team's work has been. I do know that the alternative of waiting until donations pick up again will leave hundreds of youth chronically homeless. We have the opportunity to change that, and I hope we do."

"Well said, Chuck," offered Michael. "As you can see from the risk assessment analysis, having the support of the ad hoc committee is a critical milestone for us. We want you to keep us grounded with your comments, helping, also, to keep us from making mistakes, but we *do* hope you're supportive of our social enterprise initiative."

"I think the committee is supportive," said Howard. "Initially when we met before the planning even started, I was afraid of mission creep. You've convinced me that we're hitting the bull's eye of our mission—developing productive citizens. I believe we're on track for a successful initiative."

"Well, I guess I'm the odd person out," inserted Kathy. "I *don't* think this is what we should be doing, and if the rest of you are going to vote for this, then I'm in the wrong place."

"We haven't heard from everyone, Kathy. Why don't we keep going?"

"No thanks. I've heard enough. I'll be tendering my resignation to Curt tomorrow. Goodbye." Kathy collected her things and exited the room, leaving the other members shaking their heads, wondering what just happened.

Sarah sat down. Howard stood up. "Let's take a fifteen minute breather to collect ourselves while I call and update Curt. Then we can talk about where we go from here. Amazing."

Renewed Commitment

Curt held a closed-door session with Howard and Michael. Then he called a meeting with Jason and the ad hoc board committee. "I am reluctantly accepting Kathy's resignation from the NextPlace4Good board. I've spoken with her and emphasized how much we appreciate contrary views, even conflict. I encouraged her to stay on the board and the ad hoc committee. She feels strongly, however, that we should *not* be planning a new venture. I couldn't convince her to stay on as devil's advocate so we benefit from her opposing perspective. So now I want each of you to tell me *honestly* if you think we're on the wrong track or being fiscally irresponsible. This is the time to speak up. I'm asking everyone to be brutally candid."

Julia began: "Curt, from what I can tell, we're on a right track. If we're not able to raise the money to get this venture going, then this might be a waste. But it's too early to know."

Chuck added, "I agree with Julia. It's too early, and we haven't gone far enough to really vet this idea and our plan. Kathy's reaction wasn't called for, in my view. I see Michael being a great mentor to Jason. And Jason is really developing his leadership just as we had hoped. Sarah is bringing us a process and taking us step-by-step toward a go/no-go decision."

"Absolutely, Curt," said Darren. "I wish we did this type of thorough analysis at my company when we're about to develop a new product. I hope I'm not being naïve, but it definitely feels like we're on solid ground. I think there's a mountain of work still to do, but that's always true, isn't it?"

"I've been through the nightmare of reducing our services," observed Jason, "and maybe even closing our doors. Although this venture has lots of risks, which nobody is denying, it holds the promise of a more reliable revenue source and new opportunities for our clients. The time investment to do this plan may be the hardest on me since I also have to accomplish my regular duties. But I find a way to do both because the promise of financial sustainability energizes me and makes me optimistic about the future of NextPlace4Good's clients."

"There you have it, Curt," Howard summarized. "Michael and I shared our views and support for this with you earlier. How do you want to proceed?"

"Wait," said Michael. "As I told Curt, I think we are right on target. I want to share with all of you that our planning included a field trip to a nonprofit in Tucson that went through this exact process. Not only did they succeed with their initial venture, in the span of a year, they had built their competence and confidence to the point of launching *two new* ventures. And I doubt they will stop there as long as they see ways to expand their earned income, develop employment and training for their clients, and better fulfill their mission. Like all of you have said, it's too early to declare victory, but this certainly feels like a better solution than Jason's nightmare scenario. That's all."

Curt then offered his viewpoint: "Thank you all. I feel much the same and don't understand why Kathy took such a harsh stand against the venture. Nevertheless, what I'm going to do next is ask Matt to join the ad hoc committee. His degree is in business. Until we get another CPA on our board, he can add a financial dimension to the committee. That will help keep us on schedule while our Governance Committee looks for a replacement for Kathy. Let me thank you all for your input, as well as for the extra commitment to serve on this committee. Again, you've all been very positive and supportive. It's great to hear. I've heard it said that you couldn't make an omelet without breaking some eggs. In other words, it's more important to speak up if you see something that doesn't make sense, or that's not fiscally responsible, or that the team just plain missed. I would hope we would not need to take the all-or-nothing stand that Kathy did, but it is required that you speak up and make your views known, however contrary. Are we good with that?"

"Yes!" they all agreed in unison, and the meeting ended.

Snatching Defeat from the Jaws of Victory

Matt was flattered and pleased to join the ad hoc committee. He dedicated an afternoon to reading the business plan and developing his questions for Jason. Meanwhile, Jason had received a call from David Willis, a program manager at the Hercules Foundation. David had heard about the proposed social venture and was eager to explain their foundation's social entrepreneurship funding. Of course, Jason was most interested in hearing about start-up funding and was thrilled to learn from David when they met that the foundation could almost guarantee a $100,000 start-up grant. Jason took the initiative to complete the request and keep in touch with daily calls to David. This was almost too good to pass up. He was pumped up that financing would be arranged at the same time their business plan was presented to the board.

That was the next milestone—a meeting of the full board to review the business plan and vote to proceed.

The core team worked almost full-time polishing the business plan wording and developing the financial models using different scenarios. They looked at their risk analysis and talked about what could go wrong, building a financial model of the "worst case" scenario. They developed a "green lights through town" scenario as a best case. With these as the outside boundaries, they spent most of their time working the "realistic" scenario to include in their official business plan.

At one of their work sessions, Jason mentioned he had met with the Hercules Foundation. Sarah and Michael encouraged his initiative. Sarah said, "It's a positive recognition of our work that Hercules is interested in our social venture." The team focused on getting the financial model completed. Jason's teammates assumed that discussions with Hercules were preliminary. They weren't focused on probing how far the discussions had progressed. Jason made the assumption that his advisors approved of his actions and that he should continue.

The start-up expenses had been systematically identified, and in many instances, validated by comparisons with the experiences of others. To account for contingencies, they debated whether to include five percent or ten percent of total costs as contingent. Feeling confident in their detail, they selected five percent for contingencies.

The morning of the board meeting, the team practiced their presentation. Jason announced he had secured start-up funding from Hercules. He took both Sarah and Michael by total surprise. Michael asked, "That would be great. I had no idea they were really serious. Have they made a written commitment to us?"

"Not yet, but David has been very positive and says putting something in writing is a formality."

"Oh, well, do you really want to be that definitive to the board at this meeting? I mean, mentioning that we're beginning the discussions and that we've received a positive response from one foundation seems appropriate. But without written confirmation, don't we run the risk of overstating our situation?"

"No, Michael, I'm telling you that I've been working with David Willis on a continuing basis. The funding is going to happen. This isn't overstating. I think assuring them we have secured start-up funding from a foundation will ease board member minds, especially if anyone has financial concerns like Kathy's before she stormed out."

Michael shrugged his shoulders and acquiesced.

The board meeting went swimmingly. The business plan was well written. The team explained their plans in detail, and the ad hoc committee did their job, voicing strong support for the plan, as well as the team's work. When they reviewed the financial model, Jason disregarded the caution of his two main advisors, proclaiming victory in securing the necessary start-up funding through Hercules.

Curt exclaimed, "That's wonderful news. I wasn't anticipating it would be that easy. Great job, Jason. We'll be on our way in no time." Michael and Sarah exchanged a look, but they kept quiet, not wanting to put a damper on Jason's biggest presentation.

Other board members chimed in with their congratulatory comments and effusive praise. It couldn't have gone better—the smiles and compliments went on and on.

That evening Jason felt relieved and tired as the adrenaline rush faded. He and Polly enjoyed a relaxing dinner at home and toasted a glass of wine to the future success of NextPlace4Good. Although he slept a little later the next morning, Jason was anxious to get to the office and meet with his program director, Alicia, to get organized for the next phase. A phone message from David was waiting on Jason's desk. He was eager to share the positive reception from the board with Hercules Foundation.

David's voice was anything but excited. He broke the news: "Jason, my boss refused to bring your grant application forward. He says we need to get some other funding sources to step up first, and then *maybe* he'll bring the topic up to the trustees. Sorry to be the bearer of bad news, but I think that means we're out of the picture for now."

"*What?* That can't be David! I had your word, and I told the board it was a sure thing. You cannot be serious!"

"I'm really, really sorry, Jason. I tried to talk to him and say how good your plan was, but couldn't convince him to go for it. When he makes up his mind, it's almost impossible to get him to change it."

The weak-kneed young man slumped into his office chair. Head in hands, he worked to fight the panic setting in. It was all so clear now—Michael's cautionary advice—Jason had nothing in writing. He hadn't even been dealing with the decision-maker. What would the board think of him now that he had to snatch defeat from the jaws of victory?

He knew he wasn't thinking clearly. Ideas weren't coming to him, just a mantra of guilt for not listening to his trusted advisors, anger at himself for being so blind to reality, and most of all, dread about the discussion he would now be forced to have with Michael, Sarah and members of his board.

Jason quietly slipped out of the building to take a long walk through the neighborhood. At first, his anxiety grew worse as he considered whether he had put the whole initiative in jeopardy. After awhile, Jason calmed down and ideas began to form. He still feared he might be fired—or at least demoted. But eventually, he'd cleared the emotion enough to find a bench in the park and sit down to make notes.

1. Call Michael first – remember to apologize!
2. Call Curt and ask how he wants to communicate to board.
3. Do it.

Michael listened to Jason's confession. "Look, Jason, this isn't the end of the world. This isn't what we wanted, but we have to remember what's important and keep that in perspective. The important part is that we have a dynamite business plan. We didn't expect the funding would be handed to us on a silver platter—certainly not so easily. Consider this a learning experience. I'll go with you to talk to Curt."

"No Michael, I appreciate the offer, but I screwed this up, so it's my task to tell Curt. I appreciate your help, especially putting this in perspective. I certainly haven't been able to on my own. Would you call Sarah though? That would help."

"Of course I will. I also want to remind you that we're going in front of an audience of social investors in three weeks in San Francisco. We need to focus on your presentation and hone it. Again, not assuming that our start-up expenses will magically appear, but it's another chance to tell our story, hear investor questions and concerns, and then address them in our plan. Eventually, practicing our pitch to potential investors will pay off for us. Do you believe me, Jason?"

"Yeah, I guess so. Thanks, Michael. I'll call you after I call Curt. Wish me luck."

Michael sat back in his chair after the call. He remembered a leadership story he had once heard. A young employee made a colossal, costly mistake in a project that cost his company hundreds of thousands of dollars. He was called in to his manager's office, imagining he would be fired. Instead, the manager calmed the talented, but highly upset employee by telling him the company had just invested $250,000 in his development and learning. The important thing was to learn from the experience and put the learning to good use. Michael decided he should call Jason again and tell him that story.

SECTION 7:
Business Plan: Financing the Social Enterprise

Meet the Impact Investors

The team was at the Fort Mason Center in San Francisco for the conference. Sarah and Michael were helping Jason to calm himself before his presentation. Over one thousand social entrepreneurs, investors and advocates were at this year's Social Capital Market conference. Jason had received a scholarship to come and had his charts ready for his ten-minute presentation to an audience and a panel of impact investors. By far, this was the largest audience he had ever addressed, and in his mind, the highest stakes he'd ever played for.

"Just be yourself, Jason," said Michael. "This audience wants you to succeed. And we'll get additional feedback on our plan while there's still plenty of time to adjust for their comments. This is a terrific opportunity for us. You're ready and well prepared, buddy!"

"I know, I know, but I'm still nervous. How's my tie?"

"Fine, you look fine. This is San Francisco. You're the most formally dressed person at the conference."

"Should I take it off?"

"No, I was just making a joke. Sarah, did you talk with the audio-visual folks? Are our PowerPoint slides loaded up?"

"All set, Michael. Nothing to it, but to do it. This workshop will be well attended. Whenever people arrive early to get a good seat, you know there'll be a crowd. Wouldn't it be great if there were some Arizona folks in the room? Oh, they're calling for you, Jason, so you can meet the panelists before your presentation."

The three panel members and moderator were seated behind a table on the stage at an angle so that both the audience and the speaker at the podium could see them. The three presenting entrepreneurs were seated behind the podium. In addition to Jason, one young man had launched a software company for schools after his two-year Teach for America assignment.

"Great to meet you, Aaron." said Jason. "We studied Teach for America as part of our strategic meeting this year. I became a great fan of the organization. Good luck today."

"Thanks. You, too, Jason."

"We now invite Jason Greene to the podium. Jason is the CEO of NextPlace4Good and will be presenting a new social enterprise business plan to employ clients in an urban garden and sell the crops at local Farmer's Markets. Please welcome Jason!"

After the applause, Jason began his presentation. "Good morning and thank you for the chance to share an exciting opportunity for our organization. NextPlace4Good works with homeless youth, ages seventeen to twenty-four, helping them become productive citizens in our community. We have developed a business plan to train and employ selected clients to plant and grow a garden that will become a source of revenue for our clients working as employees, as well as revenue for the organization itself.

At first, we plan to sell produce from our garden through existing Farmer's Markets, but shortly, we will create a Farmer's Market of our own, located in a low income community where fresh produce is not readily available."

Jason then provided a brief overview of the business plan: "I will first highlight our Market Analysis to show that our targeted consumer segment is ready and able to support the produce sales goals we have set. Then I will highlight key elements of our initiative to capture this market segment profitably. Finally, I will outline the start-up investments and the planned financial growth of our venture over a three-year time frame." After fleshing out additional details for his audience of potential investors, Jason concluded by thanking them for the opportunity to present his organization's social enterprise venture.

Of the three review panelists, the representative from Capital for Good provided the most specific feedback about NextPlace4Good's enterprise. This reviewer observed that although the team had been conservative in sales growth, he wondered if they needed to consider seasonality more seriously and allow for a larger fall-off in summer sales during Phoenix's extreme heat. The other two review panelists suggested contacts and connections for Jason who might help him. These three reviewers' comments and suggestions were very helpful to the team, but the biggest surprise happened after the workshop.

Victory!

On his first day back in Phoenix, Jason was pumped up. In fact, he couldn't sleep, so he got dressed and went to the office. Jason thought he'd be the early bird, but a number of cars were already parked in the parking lot. Well, he thought, that's good because I'll be able to share our good news. Entering the lobby, he was met by laughter and cooing. His staff was surrounding a woman holding an infant. "Wait," he thought, "is that who I think it is? *Yes, Malaika! She's had her baby!*"

Jason reflected on how quickly time had passed since his first meeting with Michael when Malaika had come looking for baby clothes.

"Jason!" Alicia shouted over the crowd. "Welcome back! Come here and meet Shaniqua. She's adorable, and you won't believe our incredible luck. Malaika just earned her Associate's Degree in Business from Gateway Community College with a concentration in accounting. She's actually interested in our Business Manager position at WorkPlace4Good, the new business venture of NextPlace4Good. We could have our first hire be someone we've helped. She could even bring the baby to work most days. Oh, oops, I guess I'm getting ahead of myself. We still need funding, don't we? How could I forget? How was San Francisco?"

Jason was now holding Shaniqua on his shoulder and laughing with an ear-to-ear grin. "Malaika, she is beautiful! I feel so experienced now that I've been a dad for five months. Listen up everyone. I have such wonderful news I can hardly hold it in anymore."

"I made my presentation—nerves and all. It was mostly a blur, but Michael and Sarah said I did fine. Personally, I don't remember speaking. The panel members were all big shots from social venture funds. I enjoyed meeting them. They offered great advice, assistance and even contacts. But—and this I didn't really expect—after the workshop was over, five Arizona participants crowded around me. Two of them were from local foundations. I have their cards, and they wanted to congratulate us on our good work so far. They even want us to call them to talk more about what we're up to with the garden and Farmer's Market. That was gratifying. Three of them came from Social Venture Partners Arizona, and they committed to funding our initial start-up costs for the garden—the whole $100,000. Woohoo! Just like that, they made a decision and will be here later today!"

"Malaika," exclaimed Alicia, "You may have a job before you realize it."

SECTION 8:
Epilogue

Field Trip – Others Learn From Us

Three years have passed. Jason and Michael are waiting in the conference room for Sarah to arrive. She is bringing a new client who has engaged her to help write their business plan. The enterprise would employ their autism spectrum clients in a janitorial enterprise. Sarah asks if Jason and Michael will share their perspective on the business planning process and their lessons learned from the start-up.

"Hi Sarah!" They both jumped up and hugged her when she entered the conference room. "It's been too long since we've gotten together. We miss you!" Jason exclaimed.

"I miss you both—and the team, as well," said Sarah. "I'm also delighted at how great you're doing. I feel very proud to have participated in the planning process of your WorkPlace4Good venture."

Turning to the man and woman by her side, Sarah said, "I'd like to introduce you to Steven McDonald, CEO of Unlimited Futures, and the Unlimited Futures board chair, Susan Roth. We have looked at the Market Opportunity for commercial janitorial services as a workforce development strategy for their clients in the autism spectrum. Jason, it would be great if you could recap what we did and give Steve and Sue a chance to ask questions."

"Absolutely!" Jason said with enthusiasm. "Just stop me any time with your questions." Then he proceeded to explain how they had planned and financed their garden and Farmer's Market, concluding by providing Sarah and her clients an update on the social enterprise venture's current status.

"Our Farmer's Market officially launched eighteen months ago. Up to that point, we were ramping up our urban garden and recruiting vendors. We followed the business plan pretty religiously. We had enough start-up funding to cover our cash flow deficit for the first two years. This third year, we've been on our own. It's been a touch-and-go challenge, but we'll close the year at a breakeven."

Steve, CEO of Unlimited Futures, wanted to learn from their undertaking, so he asked, "What would you have done differently with 20-20 hindsight?"

"Well, except for being overly optimistic about our first funding source," Michael winked at Jason who turned beet red, "I can't think of much we would do differently. Can you Jason?"

"Not in the planning process anyway. The process Sarah uses covers all the bases. It also forced us to really discuss every aspect of the enterprise as a team. As we talked through our ideas while developing our written plan, we found a way to sequence our business development and get a good grip on each stage before we pursued the next one. It still felt like we were going 180 miles an hour, but we were focused on the success of each stage: first getting our staff trained for gardening, then selling produce and fruit at two existing Farmer's Markets, then recruiting vendors for our own market."

Michael concluded, "It's the old adage. The more we planned, the smarter we got."

"Well, what has surprised you most then?" asked Susan of Unlimited Futures.

"I think two things have been a real surprise," Jason continued. "The first surprise is that the Farmer's Market has become an important community place. It's what I'd hoped for, but it's even better. In addition to an active produce marketplace, neighborhood families come for Saturday lunch at the Bar-B-Q grill. They actually stay to visit and listen to the musicians, who are happy for an audience. The music was added when a music therapy nonprofit provided instruments to NextPlace4Good clients. Our clients immediately formed a performing band."

"The second surprise was our turnover. It's been twice as high as we expected. We planned for our employee clients to get training and stay for two years. With the Master Gardener training and retail produce experience, they've become eligible for much better jobs after only one year. Even though they come back and volunteer with us, it's forced us to become very efficient in our workforce training and job training."

"That's not all bad, is it?" Susan asked.

"It's not bad at all. I have the statistics here. The year before we launched our enterprise, we had twelve clients earn their GED and forty-one clients get jobs and permanent housing. This year we've grown the GED numbers to thirty, the clients with jobs and housing to seventy-five. So while it was a surprise to us, that type of turnover is terrific because it demonstrates success, rather than failure. And the young people who have succeeded have become great role models in the community, as well as for all our clients. We are still mindful that we're only serving a small number of homeless youth compared to the total population in our mission."

Michael interrupted, "So mindful, in fact, that the board and Jason are relooking at our strategic goals and developing five-year goals that will grow our successes by the hundreds. To be followed by the next five-year plan with successes in the thousands. And these goals will drive us to develop more WorkPlace4Good enterprises that employ our clients, as well as fund the organization."

"Both of those surprises are wonderful outcomes!" Susan laughed. "I hope we are surprised in that way in our venture."

"Susan, as Board Chair, you'll appreciate how much it's meant to all the board members to have a more sustainable business model," Michael added. "Our revenue is now twenty percent earned income, from almost zero before we started."

And Jason piped in, "Melons to Money! Sarah came up with that ditty when we first decided on the urban garden. That's when the light bulb went on for me. We had started to think about a new business model—a market based enterprise to help more clients and our organization at the same time. So growing melons—and peppers and peas, serves our mission and gives us a predictable, sustainable source of money. You get the idea!"

They all laughed, and the visitors from Unlimited Futures were grateful for the insights from NextPlace4Good's experience, especially about how staff and board members from their nonprofit could embark on their own journey toward a thriving social enterprise.

PART 2:

COMPLETED DOCUMENTS AND BUSINESS PLAN

NextPlace4Good

ACTION LOG: For Review January 23

<u>Goal:</u> $100,000 annual improvement in Profit and Loss Statement achieved within 60 days through a combination of expense reduction and additional revenue.

Date Assigned	Action with Expected Results	Assigned To	Complete Date	Complete YES/NO	Impact Estimate	Impact Actual	Comment
1/16	Move Adam to part time position	Adams	2/15	YES	$ 24,500	$24,500	Salary + benefits
1/16	Rent computer room to others	Adams	~~3/15~~ REV: 4/15	NO	$ 15,000		Will meet revised date
1/16	Renegotiate lease	Greene	3/15	NO	$ 10,000		Might be $8,000
1/16	Further reduce discretionary expenses	Adams	2/20	YES	$ 5,500	$5,000	Will try to increase to $7,000
1/16	Apply to local foundations for emergency funds	Greene	3/15	NO	$ 15,000	$7,500	Have had 4 meetings – in process
1/16	Solicit repeat donors to increase donation	Greene + board	~~3/15~~ REV: 4/15	NO	$ 20,000	$9,000	Working on Top 50 list, including board
1/16	Defer payments to vendors	Adams	1/31	YES	$ 5,000	$4,000	Not permanent
1/16	Close alternate Fridays	Adams	1/31	YES	$ 2,500	$3,000	For 90 days
1/16	Employee paid holiday party	Adams	1/16	YES	$ 2,500	$2,500	Budget reduction

Date Assigned	Action with Expected Results	Assigned To	Complete Date	Complete YES/NO	Impact Estimate	Impact Actual	Comment
1/23	Additional $ for consultant	Greene	2/15	NO	($ 3,000)	($3,000)	Facilitate strategic retreat
1/23	Unidentified savings	Greene	2/15	NO	$ 5,000		
				TOTALS	$102,000	$52,500	

NextPlace4Good
Strategic Planning Retreat
External Environmental Trends

TOPIC	RELEVANT TRENDS
Economic	*The Phoenix area economy - reached bottom but recovering very slowly compared to cities in other parts of the country. *The historical population growth of the Phoenix area slowing. The projected annual growth rate for the next decade 2.0% - 2.6%. *Joblessness is also worse in Phoenix than other cities, greatly affecting the lower skilled labor base. Arizona was ranked 2nd in the nation for job growth before the great recession. Arizona's rank descended to 49th during the recession as the combination of construction, retail, semiconductor, tourism and retirement losses eliminated 1 job in 11. *The job recovery will extend slowly over many years.
Societal	*Divisiveness and polarization in views of government spending for social services. *Lack of education and skills lead to long-term unemployment as economy falters and unskilled jobs less abundant. *Immigration and illegal immigration a front burner, emotional issue.
Technology	*Tools for communications, information, business operations, entertainment, etc. continue to advance at ever more affordable cost.
Governmental	*Serious state and local spending reductions in social and health services.
Homelessness	*Homelessness overall has taken a turn for the worse because of housing foreclosures; family homelessness was a potential impact for NextPlace4Good as homeless children become teens.
Tax Exempt (nonprofits) + Donors/ Funders	*Collective Impact of many organizations being deployed to solve difficult issues, including homelessness. *Partnerships and alliances considered as a minimum. *Alliance of AZ Nonprofits 2012 nonprofit survey: "Borderline: Hope and Concern for Arizona Nonprofits." Findings include: About 45 percent of nonprofits will have to reduce their budgets in 2012 and nearly 30 percent expect to end 2012 with a deficit. Revenue losses are moderating. The mean decrease in nonprofit revenue was 16 percent in 2011, down from 18 percent in 2010 and 22 percent in 2009. Arts and culture nonprofits continue to suffer most as donors are choosing to give to human services organizations instead. According to the report, 44 percent of Arizona nonprofits lost some government funding in 2011 and 24 percent lost some corporate support. Nonprofit leaders expect this trend to continue in 2012. Some nonprofits are still feeling the effect of the decline in government funding as well as continuing to keep carving out their space in the private philanthropy world. It's difficult because there are a lot of appeals out there. At least half of Arizona nonprofits are tapping into their financial reserves to stay afloat, and most of those have fewer than four months of operating reserves available, the report found.

NextPlace4Good
SWOT Analysis

Strengths	Weaknesses
• Staff and management dedication • Staff and management competence • Track record of results and success stories • Committed board • Good community relations • Clients value services provided in holistic manner	• Financial security • Overworked staff • Facility needs updating • Lack of employment opportunities for clients due to recession • Insufficient community resources to meet all client needs
Opportunities	**Threats**
• "Un-captured Market" as many as 18,000 homeless youth in area • "Alumni" base as supporters • Job training, skill-building and job creation for working age homeless youth • Earned Income from business that employs homeless youth – some clients currently earn stipends for work at supportive housing • Phoenix area collective impact initiative to end homelessness and build supportive housing	• Government budget deficits restrain funding • Recession causing more homeless youth • Slow economic recovery with unforeseen disruptions • Slow growing economy means slow growing donations

NextPlace4Good
Analysis of Possible Social Enterprises
Assigning points to each criterion

Opportunity	Fits SWOT Strengths	Fits SWOT Opportunities	Low Start up $	High $ Revenue Potential	Work Training for clients	High Market Need	TOTAL
Points	0-20	0-10	0-15	0-15	0-25	0-15	0-100
Commercial buildings janitorial services	15	10	10	5	10	0	50
Bakeries that sell retail and wholesale	20	5	5	10	15	10	65
Landscaping and lawn maintenance	20	10	10	5	15	5	65
Assembly or sub assembly as contract manufacture	20	5	5	10	15	10	65
Basic work like making pizza boxes or shredding documents	15	5	10	0	5	5	40
Laundry and dry cleaning	5	5	5	5	10	5	35
Restaurants and coffee shops	5	5	0	5	15	5	35
Community gardens	20	10	10	10	20	10	80
Art galleries	5	5	5	5	5	5	30
Repair work on HVAC units, appliances, electronics	10	10	5	15	25	10	75

NextPlace4Good
Urban Garden & Farmer's Market
Business Plan

I. Executive Summary

NextPlace4Good, a 501(c)(3) tax exempt organization serving homeless youth ages seventeen to twenty-four, has developed this social enterprise plan to produce a *triple bottom line*: (1) employment for its qualified clients, (2) healthy fresh food in a low income neighborhood without a nearby grocery store, and (3) profitability after two years to reinvest in its mission.

The wholly owned, for-profit subsidiary, WorkPlace4Good, will hire and train clients as Master Gardeners for an urban garden where fresh produce will be sold as one vendor of many in a Farmer's Market, owned and operated by WorkPlace4Good. Supervised by an external hire for the garden and market—along with an external hire as Business Manager for inventory management, cash control and budget management—up to twenty clients will be trained over the three-year planning period.

The community will reap the benefits of up to ten fresh food vendors, including WorkPlace4Good. Produce prices, freshness and quantity will approximate that of a major grocery store because there is none located in this low income community in Phoenix, classified as a "food desert." The market will accept EBT payments from government food programs, WIC and SNAP. The local farms will benefit from direct sales to consumers, an additional sales outlet of interest that they estimate to be profitable.

The start-up funding requirements and working capital requirements (prior to positive cash flow) are estimated at $140,000. Additionally we will secure a workforce development grant of $25,000 and approximately $10,000 of in-kind equipment. The board of NextPlace4Good will dedicate $40,000 of the start-up funding from its net assets reserve. The board will seek to raise the final $100,000 from social investors.

The business plan first describes the overall market opportunity and then specifies the target market segment for this venture. The initiative to serve the market opportunity is then described in depth, including where there are gaps to fill. Mitigation actions to identified risks are described. The final section summarizes the financial model and key performance indicators to monitor progress.

The board and staff of NextPlace4Good believe this venture will be successful according to this plan. Success will encourage a proliferation of additional future social enterprises and employment opportunities.

II: The Market Opportunity

The market opportunity to produce and sell affordable fresh produce will first be described in general to define its overall characteristics. Then, specific market segments will be identified. Finally, a targeted segment will be identified for this business plan. The goal is to identify a need that NextPlace4Good can satisfy through an urban garden and Farmer's Market in a neighborhood that currently has limited access to affordable, fresh produce, known as a food desert.

Overall Market Size and Growth Rates – This section covers size, growth and additional characteristics for low income neighborhoods with limited supermarket access for food-at-home purchases and for Farmer's Markets as the retail outlet under consideration. These three dimensions are described for the U.S. as a whole and the local Maricopa County (greater Phoenix AZ metropolitan area).

Food Deserts U.S. – U.S.D.A. Definition (See Appendix I of the business plan for additional description from U.S.D.A. website): "There are many ways to define a food desert or to measure access to food. The Economic Research Service's (ERS) Food Desert Locator is based on a definition developed by USDA, Treasury, and HHS. Low-income census tracts with a substantial number or share of residents with low levels of access to retail outlets selling healthy and affordable foods are defined as food deserts."

Food Deserts U.S. – Size: Supermarkets and large grocery stores—defined as food stores with at least $2 million in annual sales and containing all the major food departments—are used as proxies for sources of healthy and affordable food . . . "According to these definitions and data sources, an estimated 13.5 million people in the United States have low access to a supermarket or large grocery store, with 82 percent living in urban areas."

Food Deserts - Maricopa County AZ – The 2006 U.S.D.A. Food Atlas identified 55 census tracts as food deserts where 148,588 low-income residents (~5 percent of the population) live more than one mile from a supermarket and where 11,699 of those residents do not have access to a car. Children ages 0-17 in poverty were 21.6 percent of the county population in 2010.

Food Security – Maricopa County AZ - The combination of *Food Insecure Households* averaged 15.3 percent between 2008-2010 and *Very Low Secure Households* averaged 5.9 percent, which totaled 21.2 percent of total households in the county. SNAP (Supplemental Nutrition Assistance Program) participation of the total population grew by a third between 2009 – 2011 to 16.47 percent and WIC (Women, Infants and Children Food and Nutrition Service) participation in the same period decreased a bit from 3.17 percent to 3.08 percent. Low income preschool obesity between 2008-2010 was 14.9 percent.

Food at Home Market - U.S. – As reported by the U.S.D.A. at home food expenditures in 2010 averaged $2,093 per person, growing roughly at the rate of inflation, 1-4 percent per year over the past decade. Food purchased away from home is almost as much at $1,923 per person in 2010. The majority of at home food expenditures were at supermarkets (63 percent), the second major source being warehouse clubs/supercenters at 15.8 percent of expenditures. Expenditures at farmers/wholesalers were 6 percent of the total. These expenditures exclude food purchased at restaurants and fast food places.

Another way to look at the food at home 2010 data: direct purchases by families or individuals is 82.7 percent, produced at home was 1.7 percent, expenditures through government programs such as SNAP and WIC was 6.1 percent and business purchases, including philanthropy, was 9.5 percent.

U.S.D.A. studies show the lowest income households pay .5-1.3 percent more for food than high income, although low income (vs. lowest income) households pay less.

Food at Home Market - Maricopa County AZ – The 2010 population was 3.817 million and continuing to grow but at a slower rate (1.65 percent in 2011) than the previous decade. Approximately 5 percent of the population in the county resides in a low income area more than a mile from a supermarket in a food desert. Using the federal guide for the average at home food expenditure, each food desert census tract of approximately 4,000 residents would approximate $8,400,000 of annual spending for food at home.

Farmer's Markets - U.S. – Farmer's Markets have grown rapidly as the fascination with all things local and all things fresh has become popular. The farmer sets up a stand at a regularly scheduled market and sells direct to shoppers. Depending on the market, the farmer pays a small flat fee or a commission on sales. Farmers don't have to give payment terms or wholesale prices, as they would to a store or restaurant, so more money stays in the farmer's pocket. Depending on the market, you may find yourself chatting with the farmer. The USDA's voluntary reporting of Farmer's Markets shows high growth:

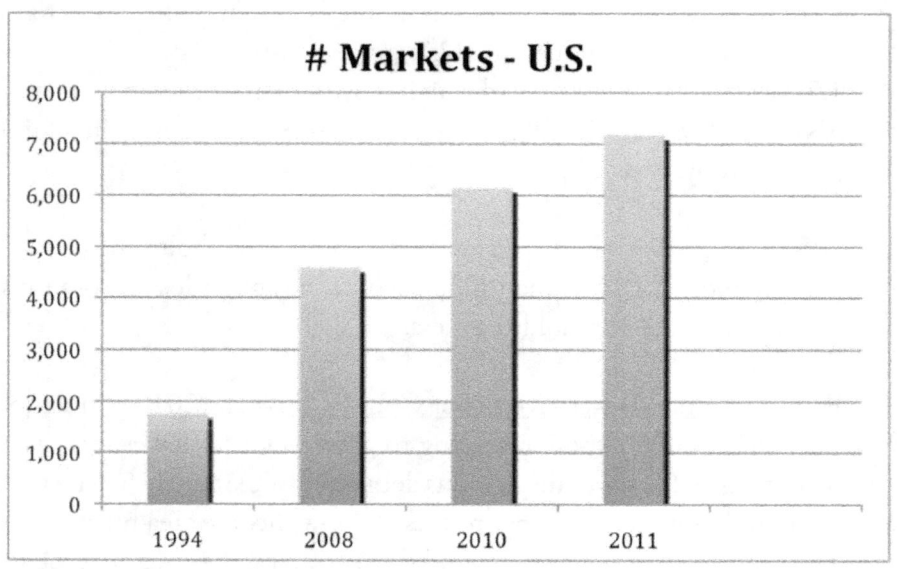

 # Markets - U.S.

<u>Farmer's Markets - Maricopa County AZ</u> – In 2011 there are 30 Farmer's Markets in Maricopa County, *none in low income communities* labeled as food deserts. Several local small farms are identified on a Local Harvest locator map within Maricopa County.

<u>Locally Grown Food – Maricopa County AZ</u> - USDA records for 2007 identify 32 vegetable farms that harvested 17,472 acres, 180 orchards with 4,080 orchard acres, 129 farms that had farm direct sales and 31 farms that grew vegetables for fresh markets.

<u>Market Segmentation</u> – Defining geographic areas with limited supermarket access and no existing Farmer's Market is the most relevant characteristic for our market. Additionally, the lack of access to a car and eligibility for government support programs plays an important role in segmentation. A listing of possible geographic areas with relevant characteristics follows:

Possible areas to locate an Urban Garden and Farmer's Market

CENSUS TRACT	TOTAL POP'N	LOW INCOME	LOW INC. + LOW ACCESS	LOW ACCESS CHILDREN	LOW ACCESS 65+	HSEHOLDS W/NO CAR	LOCATION
6203	2,120	1,507 – 71.1%	390 – 19.8%	485 – 22.9%	52 – 2.4%	8 – 1%	24th St – 40th St, Broadway – Baseline
6100	3,987	3,987 – 100%	2,076 – 52.7%	1,428 – 35.8%	171 – 4.3%	190 – 20.3%	24th St – 32nd St, Broadway – Southern
6000	4,711	1,418 – 30.1%	455 – 9.7%	495 – 10.5%	205 – 4.4%	149 – 10.5%	16th St – 24th St., Broadway – Southern
5300	2,394	1,900 – 79.4%	698 – 29.6%	661 – 27.6%	181 – 7.5%	56 – 8.8%	7th St – 24th St, Rio Salado – Broadway
4800	3,216	2,861 – 88.9%	1,530 – 48%	970 – 30.2%	289 – 9%	163 – 20.9%	19th Ave – 7th Ave, Buckeye – Broadway
4302	2,829	2,829 – 100%	2,024 – 70.1%	1,253 – 44.3%	164 – 5.8%	435 – 50.1%	19th Ave – 7th Ave, RR tracks – Buckeye
4200	2,056	2,056 – 100%	1,118 – 56%	726 – 35.3%	134 – 6.5%	182 – 37.4%	7th Ave – 7th St, RR tracks – Buckeye
2900	6,255	4,653 – 74.4%	1,764 – 28.9%	1,338 – 21.4%	243 – 3.9%	327 – 17.9%	19th Ave – 7th Ave, Interstate 60 – Van Buren
4900	2,906	2,683 – 92.3%	1,536 – 52.9%	935 – 32.2%	335 – 11.5%	470 – 49.8%	7th Ave – 7th St, Buckeye – Rio Salado
5200	3,113	3,113 – 100%	1,474 – 49.1%	1,283 – 41.2%	93 – 3%	170 – 22.5%	24th St – Interstate 143, Rio Salado – Broadway

All of these areas have at least one major thoroughfare and multiple vacant lots that could be used for a garden.

<u>Typical Economics of the Market Segment</u> – This section identifies the relevant dimensions that might influence buying at a Farmer's Market and a further clarification of the consumer need.

From the vendor's vantage point, key requirements include a good location that provides good foot traffic, a decent weather environment, including shade, and a minimum daily sales amount. The average monthly sales for a vendor across the U.S. are $1,070 per month. That should be a target for each vendor to achieve within two seasons. For beginning farmers, a Farmer's Market can be a springboard for their business, immediate cash and a direct consumer connection that enables them to act quickly, as well as adjust pricing and products. Farmers expect to pay a booth rental between $10-$15 a day or 5-8 percent of their sales.

From the consumers' vantage point, key requirements include an accessible location with attractive signage and shade, along with good variety and quality produce. Most existing Farmer's Markets in the county price their produce above supermarkets, where produce is a loss leader. But in a food desert, the pricing goal should be comparable to supermarkets, making the produce there at least 10 percent lower than what is available in the neighborhood small food stores. Typical weekly spend in a Farmer's Market averages $17.50 and our survey concludes that in a low income area, average sales can be $8.00-$9.00, especially if government EBT cards for SNAP and WIC are accepted.

As the USDA report to Congress stated, "Food has been used as a tool for community development. Projects such as Farmers' Markets, community gardens, promotion of culturally specific foods for ethnic minorities and Native Americans, local food production and promotion, youth agricultural and culinary training programs, and many other types of programs have all been implemented in a variety of settings, both urban and rural."

A Farmer's Market has a family atmosphere and can be part of Saturday entertainment. People expect music and prepared foods to accompany each market day.

Competition – Currently residents who purchase fresh produce using SNAP EBT cards travel 4.9 miles to a store. A Farmer's Market would provide a more locally accessible alternative for fresh produce. The competitive analysis is focused within the low income census tracts in our market segmentation analysis.

Fresh Produce Competitive Analysis within Food Desert Census Tracts
(scores relate to fresh foods only)

Name	Size Location Etc.	1-10 Quality Score	1-10 Availability Score	1-10 Price Score	Strength	Weakness
Xavier Market	Superette – 3,000 sq.ft. – Approx $1M annual sales	8	2	5	Convenient. Spanish speaking.	Carries only long shelf life items.
Only A Dollar	Discount store recently expanded to 16,000 sq.ft.	8	4	9	Added refrigeration for fresh and frozen foods. Price.	Fresh is largely milk, eggs, not vegetables & fruit.
Roy's Convenience	Convenience store at gas station	2	2	7	Convenience. Many customers/ day.	Food to go. Most not fresh.
Many (10) fast food outlets	National chain franchises.	7	2	7	Many customers. Value pricing.	Limited fresh selection. Mostly salads.
WorkPlace4Good Farmer's Market	1 acre garden, 10 vendor stall market place	10	6	8	EBT accepted. Convenient, fun, educational	Promotional marketing

Possible disruptive events, either positive or negative – On the positive side, funding to distribute healthy foods in food deserts has been accelerating with a national goal to eliminate food deserts by 2017. This trend can assist a venture with both financial resources and also the publicity to make our Farmer's Market part of a larger community solution.

There may be additional competition from major supercenter and national drug chains that are making public commitments to enter low income communities to be part of the national solution. This enables supercenters (with low prices and average 25,000 square feet of grocery space) to open in urban areas where previously their interest created pushback from city councils and protesters. National drug store chains (average grocery store square footage of 1,600 square feet) are committing to expand their selection of fresh foods in their food desert locations.

As the economics of health care are debated, there appears to be a larger role for healthy eating and active living. This may prove to be a trend, although how it might affect this venture is not yet clear.

Our targeted market within the overall market opportunity – Our target is selected with three tiers, giving us a primary, secondary and tertiary source of customers. Tier 1 census tracts are the primary geographic target segment. The selection criteria includes only tracts in low supermarket access areas and is refined to select several adjacent census tracts that will provide a sufficient customer base for both EBT and retail purchases: a significant low income base, a significant family with children base, and a high percentage (>20 percent) without a car factored into the selection. Tier 1, our geographic target, has an additional advantage of a central location on a major thoroughfare at 7th Avenue and Buckeye Road. The target segments are shown in a table and then in a visual display.

CENSUS TRACT	TOTAL POP'N	LOW INCOME	LOW INC. + LOWACCESS	LOW ACCESS CHILDREN	LOW ACCESS 65+	HSEHOLDS W/NO CAR	LOCATION
4302 TIER	2,829	2,829 – 100%	2,024 – 70.1%	1,253 – 44.3%	164–5.8%	435 – 50.1%	19th Ave – 7th Ave, RR tracks – Buckeye
#1 4200	2,056	2,056 – 100%	1,118 – 56%	726 – 35.3%	134–6.5%	182 – 37.4%	7th Ave – 7th St, RR tracks – Buckeye
4800 TIER	3,216	2,861 – 88.9%	1,530 – 48%	970 – 30.2%	289 – 9%	163 – 20.9%	19th Ave – 7th Ave, Buckeye – Broadway
#2 2900	6,255	4,653 – 74.4%	1,764 – 28.9%	1,338 – 21.4%	243–3.9%	327 – 17.9%	19th Ave – 7th Ave, Interstate 60 – Van Buren
4900 TIER #3	2,906	2,683 – 92.3%	1,536 – 52.9%	935 – 32.2%	335–11.5%	470 – 49.8%	7th Ave – 7th St, Buckeye – Rio Salado

NextPlace4Good
Farmer's Market
Target Market Segmentation

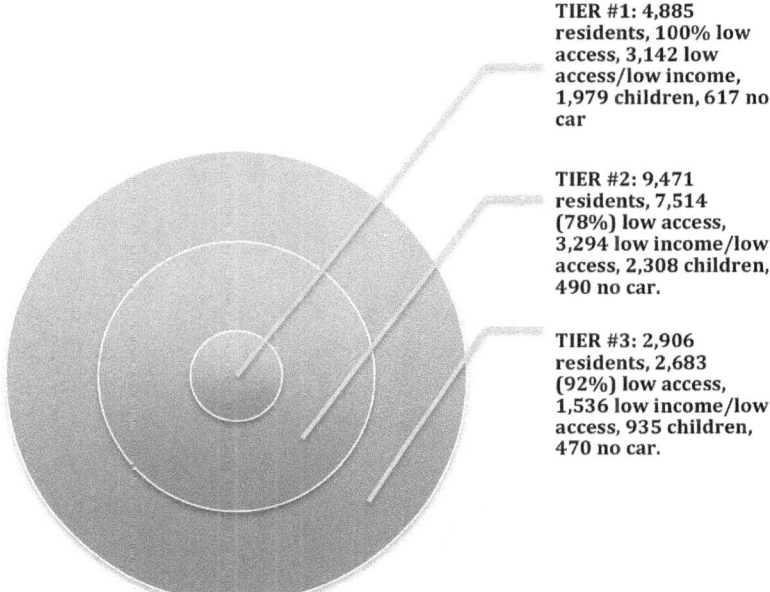

TIER #1: 4,885 residents, 100% low access, 3,142 low access/low income, 1,979 children, 617 no car

TIER #2: 9,471 residents, 7,514 (78%) low access, 3,294 low income/low access, 2,308 children, 490 no car.

TIER #3: 2,906 residents, 2,683 (92%) low access, 1,536 low income/low access, 935 children, 470 no car.

The three tiers combined residential population of over 17,000 can easily sustain a Farmer's Market with the required weekly traffic and spending. The food at home expenditure approximates $35 million with a potential 6 percent or $2 million for Farmer's Markets and wholesale sales. To capitalize on this market opportunity requires serving the EBT and retail population with the availability, quality and price combination that is lacking in the neighborhood today.

In addition to the demographics, a customer survey sponsored by NextPlace4Good sampled local residents. At least 16 percent identify they have enough to eat, but not always the kind of food they want to eat. They identify the reason as lack of access.

Our survey also identified local community leaders, interested foundations and government officials who can help us build a network of support that brings customers to our market. The market research also identified local farmers interested in becoming vendors.

In summary, we have identified a market opportunity for fresh, affordable produce. We also believe we can build a successful business initiative around our target market segment.

III. Our Initiative to Provide Fresh Affordable Produce in Food Deserts

<u>Value Proposition</u>
NextPlace4Good, through its workforce development programs to be called WorkPlace4Good, grows, sells and hosts a lively community market place for affordable fresh produce accessible in a low income community where this option has not been available.

Our efforts to provide training and employment to homeless youth and our commitment to bring healthy food into the community will engage and rally support from the broader community with all types of resources.

<u>Our Offering</u>
We will build this business in stages. The sequence to develop our full business includes the following:

(1) Train client employees as Master Gardeners,
(2) Grow and harvest fresh produce in an urban garden,
(3) Clean, batch and sell this produce at existing Farmer's Markets and our own Urban Farm Stand,
(4) Launch our own Farmer's Market in our target market food desert, offering fresh produce grown by our client workforce and other vendors in a fun, educational and community-minded environment.

A future business stage when our Farmer's Market is cash flow positive could offer prepared foods for sale, using an existing commercial kitchen and sponsoring enterprising food entrepreneurs.

Business Model Design

Our initial phase of gardening and selling produce at existing Farmer's Markets will have start-up expenses. We will be hiring a gardening expert for production planning as well as training and development of our workforce. Our expert gardener will plan production that enables us to grow sufficient crops and sell what we produce with limited spoilage, shrinkage or discounting. We will also need to select a site that will serve our garden, our market and our housing for our workforce.

Additional expenses of uniforms, laundry and transportation will be considered. As we begin, we will need a part-time Business Manager to organize and maintain our recordkeeping. Start-up expenses and time to grow our revenue base will require us to raise start-up funding.

The design of our ultimate Farmer's Market business model will include a neighborhood customer base drawn from the identified Tier 1 neighborhoods of 7th Street – 19th Avenue, from the railroad tracks to Buckeye Road.

These ~ 5,000 residents, supplemented by customers from Tiers 2 and 3 (an additional 12,000 residents), will be our primary target customer base. We expect to draw 200 – 300 customers each market day. Our research shows each low income customer will spend an average of $8.75 each market day. Produce prices will need to approximate supermarket prices, which is 30 percent lower than typical Farmer's Market prices. Government SNAP and WIC subsidies need to be accommodated for the low income residents in the community.

At 200 customers per day, we can support 7 fresh produce vendors, including WorkPlace4Good as a vendor. As we grow to 300 customers per day, we can support 10-11 vendors and make it worthwhile for them to participate.

Additionally, WorkPlace4Good will earn a modest set-up and management fee from each vendor, estimated at approximately $10 each market day.

We will outsource transportation of produce from where it's grown to our market. This will be an additional expense but less than the vehicle, insurance and training required of doing it ourselves.

<u>Our implementation scope</u> - Key requirements and gaps to be filled in our implementation plan.

Marketing – For our initial stage business, we will identify specialty, ethnic produce that differentiates us at the Central Phoenix Farmer's Market. For example, we will sell okra, kale, peppers, bok choy, etc. Our tabletop will be displayed attractively with colorful, portable signage, consistent with our marketing research. Brochures on our garden will be available, as well as permanent attractive signage with street visibility at our garden site.

> Our Organizational Gap - Creative resources to develop a memorable brand, along with a logo, business name and brochures.

Management and Human Resources – The garden and Farmer's Market business will be a wholly owned social enterprise of NextPlace4Good. We have named this new entity WorkPlace4Good. Key resources involved in the business planning include:

> Jason Greene, CEO, NextPlace4Good – MSW, University of Illinois, Has worked for Cook County Employee Assistance Program and NextPlace4Good as guidance counselor prior to CEO position.

> Michael Collins – board member, NextPlace4Good, former CEO, Triplex Corp., MBA, Colorado University

> Sarah Stoneham – Social Enterprise Consultant, Foresight & Associates, MBA, Wharton School, University of Pennsylvania

> Key skill gaps to be hired - Master Gardener / Production Leader and Business Manager/Finance Manager. See Organization Capability section below.

Technology – The initial need is a general ledger package that enables us to keep financial records and do inventory management, cash controls and cost accounting. We can use our current system by setting up a separate chart of accounts.

The system will need to support our key performance indicators (KPI's) that we will develop to track our performance against our plan.

Facility – We've located several potential properties in the Tier 1 neighborhood. The most promising is at South Central Avenue on a bus route between Hadley and Tonto. An adjacent, vacant lot could be used for parking, and we could rent a vacant ranch home across the alley for our client employees. If this property doesn't work out, we have back-up plans for several others.

Other relevant implementation requirements – We will need to verify compliance with zoning restrictions and work on a legal structure that will not compromise our tax exempt status. At a high level, our implementation has been outlined; however, a complete implementation plan will be the next phase of this project once start-up funding has been arranged.

Organization capability

- This venture will be viewed separate from our nonprofit and viewed as a business, not a charity. For example, we will terminate employees not meeting their accountabilities, even if they are clients of NextPlace4Good.
- This new venture will be a separate entity, with separate management and a subset of board members in an oversight role. Board members have been serving as an oversight committee during the business planning.
- Critical skills that we must recruit for include gardening, workforce training and development, and internal control over cash.

Schedule and milestone overview

Approval to proceed	May 1
Market Opportunity Analysis	May - June
Business Plan Development	June - August
Board Business Plan Review & Approval	Sept - October
Acquire start up financing	Oct – Feb
Hire key personnel	Feb - March
Business start-up – garden, marketing, agreements	April
Opening Day	May 1

Risks, mitigation ideas and contingency plans

Risk Area	Risk Level Low/Medium/ High	Risk Factor	Contingency Plan
Market	Medium	People continue to choose fast food over fresh food	Increase marketing; enlist additional community assistance
Competition	High	Competitive backlash from existing stores	Try enlisting them as vendors
Financial Systems	Low	Misappropriation of cash	Strict inventory mgmt and cash controls
Product	Medium	Food safety issues	Insurance coverage; safety procedures
Execution	Low	Lack of resources	Additional volunteers, board assistance, client training
Capitalization	Medium	Underestimate costs, overestimate income, run out of money	Board member get-well plan, added 5% to cost estimates
Other	Low	Disruptive Employees	Expect successful screening during hiring and training. Clear HR policies in place.

IV. Financial Model and Key Performance Indicators

Initial investment assumptions – We have considered both start-up capital and expenses and working capital needs to incorporate in our financial model.

Start-up capital – Total estimated one-time start-up capital of $11,970 plus approximately $10,000 of in-kind donations. Both one-time and annual cost estimates are included in the financial model.

ITEM	ONE-TIME	ANNUAL
Land acquisition for garden + option for parking	$2,000.00 for improvements + in-kind donations	
Refrigerator, washer & dryer for house	In-kind donations	
Business incorporation and licenses, insurance	$900.00	$1,100.00
Marketing expenses	$1,500.00	$500.00
Employee training and workforce development	$5,000.00 + U.S. Workforce Investment Act Funding	$500.00
Nearby house rental + utilities	$500.00 deposits	$4,800.00
Uniforms for employees	$500.00	$500.00
Equipment costs	$1,000.00	
Sub-Total	$11,400.00	
Contingency at 5%	$570.00	
Total estimated start-up expenses	$11,970.00	
In-kind donations not included in above	$10,600.00	

Working Capital – For two years, operating costs will exceed revenues with the gap closing gradually. Total gap is estimated at $100,000 after NextPlace4Good invests $40,000, and Phoenix Rising (a local family foundation) provides a grant of $25,000. As shown in the financial pro forma, we expect to become cash flow positive soon after our second year of operation.

Key performance indicators
1. The <10 important measurements that will be monitored for success include the following:
   - Produce grown, harvested and sold vs. monthly budget
   - Shrinkage percent in each category – harvested vs. grown and sold vs. harvested
   - Monthly cash flow balance and projection
   - Customer # per week vs. growth goal
   - Vendor # per week vs. budget
   - Clients trained and employed
   - Staff turnover

2. Data accessibility - We will need to develop weekly and monthly goals and then identify data definitions and sources. The board oversight committee and management will hold a formal monthly review of progress, issues and resolutions.

FINANCIAL PRO FORMA					
BEGINNING CASH BALANCE	$140,000				
YEAR 1	**Q1**	**Q2**	**Q3**	**Q4**	**TOTAL YEAR 1**
Produce Sales		$1,200	$2,600	$3,900	$7,700
Grant Revenues	$25,000				$25,000
Other Income					
TOTAL INCOME	$25,000	$1,200	$2,600	$3,900	$32,700
Total Produce Expenses	$500	$1,000	$1,000	$1,000	$3,500
Total Personnel Expenses	$10,500	$18,500	$18,500	$20,000	$67,500
Total Sales & Marketing Expenses			$1,000	$500	$1,500
Total General & Admin Expenses	$2,300	$1,200	$1,200	$1,200	$5,900
Other Expenses	$2,400	$5,250	$3,250	$1,140	$12,040
TOTAL EXPENSES	$15,700	$25,950	$24,950	$23,840	$90,440
NET PROFIT (LOSS)	$9,300	-$24,750	-$22,350	-$18,800	-$56,600
CASH BALANCE	$149,300	$124,550	$102,200	$83,400	

YEAR 2	Q1	Q2	Q3	Q4	TOTAL YEAR 2
Produce Sales	$6,500	$13,000	$19,500	$26,500	$65,500
Grant Revenues					
Other Income			$910	$910	$1,820
TOTAL INCOME	$6,500	$13,000	$20,410	$27,410	$67,320
Total Produce Expenses	$2,150	$2,150	$2,800	$3,450	$10,550
Total Personnel Expenses	$25,000	$25,000	$26,500	$26,500	$103,000
Total Sales & Marketing Expenses	$500				$500
Total General & Admin Expenses	$2,800	$1,200	$1,200	$1,200	$6,400
Other Expenses	$1,000	$1,000	$1,000	$1,000	$4,000
TOTAL EXPENSES	$31,450	$29,350	$31,500	$32,150	$124,450
NET PROFIT (LOSS)	-$24,950	-$16,350	-$11,090	-$4,740	-$57,130
CASH BALANCE	$58,450	$42,100	$31,010	$26,270	

YEAR 3	Q1	Q2	Q3	Q4	TOTAL YEAR 3
Produce Sales	$39,000	$45,000	$50,000	$55,500	$189,500
Grant Revenues					
Other Income	$1,300	$1,300	$2,100	$2,100	$6,800
TOTAL INCOME	$40,300	$46,300	$52,100	$57,600	$196,300
Total Produce Expenses	$6,500	$7,000	$8,000	$9,000	$30,500
Total Personnel Expenses	$30,000	$35,000	$40,000	$44,000	$149,000
Total Sales & Marketing Expenses	$500	$500	$500	$500	$2,000
Total General & Admin Expenses	$4,500	$2,500	$2,500	$2,500	$12,000
Other Expenses					
TOTAL EXPENSES	$41,500	$45,000	$51,000	$56,000	$193,500
NET PROFIT (LOSS)	-$1,200	$1,300	$1,100	$1,600	$2,800
CASH BALANCE	$25,070	$26,370	$27,470	$29,070	

APPENDIX I
USDA Food Desert Definitions

Excerpted from U.S.D.A. website:

There are many ways to define a food desert or to measure access to food. The Economic Research Service's (ERS) Food Desert Locator is based on a definition developed by USDA, Treasury, and Health and Human Services. Low income census tracts with a substantial number or share of residents with low levels of access to retail outlets selling healthy and affordable foods are defined as food deserts. A census tract is a small, relatively permanent subdivision of a county that usually contains between 1,000 and 8,000 people but generally averages around 4,000 people.

Census tracts qualify as food deserts if they meet low income and low access thresholds:

Low income: a poverty rate of 20 percent or greater, or a median family income at or below 80 percent of the statewide or metropolitan area median family income;

Low access: at least 500 persons and/or at least 33 percent of the population live more than 1 mile from a supermarket or large grocery store (10 miles, in the case of rural census tracts).

Data on population and income come from the 2000 Census of Population and Housing.

Supermarkets and large grocery stores—defined as food stores with at least $2 million in annual sales and containing all the major food departments—are used as proxies for sources of healthy and affordable food. A directory of these stores was developed from a 2006 list of stores authorized to accept Supplemental Nutrition Assistance Program (SNAP) benefits, augmented by 2006 data from Trade Dimensions TDLinx (a Nielsen company), a proprietary source of individual supermarket store listings. According to these definitions and data sources, an estimated 13.5 million people in the United States have low access to a supermarket or large grocery store, with 82 percent living in urban areas.

ABOUT THE AUTHOR

Gayle Pincus is a *Social Enterprise Catalyst*, advocating and advising social entrepreneurs and enterprising nonprofits to create thriving, profitable social enterprises. In her distinguished corporate career Pincus held executive positions with two global companies, gaining expertise in the critical success factors for businesses. She spent years honing this expertise to fit the social sector. Pincus has been recognized by the Academy of Women Achievers, New York City YWCA, and is active in Social Enterprise Alliance and Social Capital Markets. She is an active member of Financial Executives International (FEI) and serves on the board of Experience Matters, a 501(c)(3) that connects talent with community. As a Faculty Associate at Arizona State University, she teaches Social Entrepreneurship to practitioners and students. Pincus has a S.M. degree from M.I.T.'s Sloan School of Management and a B.S. from the University of Illinois. She lives in Scottsdale, Arizona with her husband Steve and enjoys international travel and hiking.

www.ingramcontent.com/pod-product-compliance
Lightning Source LLC
Chambersburg PA
CBHW051510170526
45166CB00001B/472